GUINNESS WORLD RECORDS

TO THE EXTREME

Compiled by Lisa L. Ryan-Herndon

For Guinness World Records:
Laura Barrett Plunkett, Craig Glenday, and Stuart Claxton

SCHOLASTIC ·💡· REFERENCE
An Imprint of
📖SCHOLASTIC

SCHOLASTIC INC.
New York • Toronto • London • Auckland • Sydney
Mexico City • New Delhi • Hong Kong • Buenos Aires

© 2007 Guinness World Records Limited, a HIT Entertainment Limited Company.

Published by Scholastic Inc.
■SCHOLASTIC
and associated logos are trademarks and/or registered trademarks of Scholastic Inc.

ISBN 10: 0-439-86562-X   ISBN 13: 978-0-439-86562-3

Designed by Nathan Savage/Red Herring Design
Photo Research by Els Rijper
Records from the Archives of Guinness World Records

12 11 10 9 8 7 6 5 4 3 2 1   7 8 9 10 11 12 0
Printed in China
First printing, February 2007

Visit Guinness World Records at www.guinnessworldrecords.com

CONTENTS

A Record-Breaking History

The idea for Guinness World Records grew out of a question. In 1951, Sir Hugh Beaver, the managing director of the Guinness Brewery, wanted to know which was the fastest game bird in Europe — the golden plover or the grouse? Some people argued that it was the grouse. Others claimed it was the plover. A book to settle the debate did not exist until Sir Hugh discovered the knowledgeable twin brothers Norris and Ross McWhirter, who lived in London.

Like their father and grandfather, the McWhirter twins loved information. They were just kids when they started clipping interesting facts from newspapers and memorizing important dates in world history. As well as learning the names of every river, mountain range, and nation's capital, they knew the record for pole squatting (196 days in 1954), which language had only one irregular verb (Turkish), and that the grouse — flying at a timed speed of 43.5 miles per hour — is faster than the golden plover at 40.4 miles per hour.

Norris and Ross served in the Royal Navy during World War II, graduated from college, and launched their own fact-finding business called McWhirter Twins, Ltd. They were the perfect people to compile the book of records that Sir Hugh Beaver searched for yet could not find.

The first edition of *The Guinness Book of Records* was published on August 27, 1955, and since then has been published in 37 languages and more than 100 countries. In 2000, the book title changed to *Guinness World Records* and has set an incredible record of its own: Excluding non-copyrighted books such as the Bible and the Koran, *Guinness World Records* is the bestselling book of all time!

Today, the official Keeper of the Records keeps a careful eye on each Guinness World Record, compiling and verifying the greatest the world has to offer — from the fastest and the tallest to the slowest and the smallest, with everything in between.

To the Extreme!

Can excellence be timed, measured, and weighed?

Ask Guinness World Records, the leading authority in taking the measure of excellence in years and seconds, miles and inches, tons and ounces — all for our information, astonishment, and enjoyment.

For more than half a century, these official keepers of the records have tracked, documented, and certified attempts made in every category, species, and field imaginable. Today, over 40,000 fascinating facts and unforgettable achievements by people, animals, minerals, vegetables, and mechanicals are stored inside their extensive archives.

This collection focuses on the sensational efforts of record-holders who went beyond the average and to the extreme in setting and breaking a Guinness World Record.

EXTREME

SKILLS

Every day, record-breakers cross the line between ordinary and **EXTRAORDINARY.** These superstars perfected their skills and timing to exceed all expectations!

FASTEST SANDWICH MADE BY HUMAN FEET

It is considered good manners to wash up before dining. As the record-holder for **FASTEST SAND-WICH MADE BY HUMAN FEET**, Rob Williams of Austin, Texas, scrubs his toes and soles before and *after* picking up a fork and knife. Rob demonstrated his extraordinary sand-wich-making skills during the TV show *Guinness World Records: Primetime* on November 10, 2000. His adept toes stacked a bologna-and-cheese sand-wich in 1 minute 57 seconds — and he didn't hold the lettuce, tomatoes, or pickles!

"It's a pretty good sand-wich, if you can get over the way it was created," Rob claims. Anyone want a bite?

TRIVIA TIDBITS
A "sole-full" sandwich has two slices of bread (taken out of the loaf packet in the time limit), Oscar Mayer bologna (rind peeled off), slices of square processed cheese (plastic removed), lettuce, sliced tomatoes, mustard, mayonnaise, and sliced pickles. Add olives on cocktail sticks, cut in half, then place on a plate!

DID YOU KNOW?
Rob Williams was "Gyro" of The Flaming Idiots, a juggling trio skilled in fire, knife, and comedic stunts.

MOST TOE WRESTLING WORLD CHAMPIONSHIP WINS

In 1976, the sport of toe wrestling pushed off at Ye Olde Royal Oak Inn located in Wetton, UK. Today, the sport has sprouted in popularity among all ages, and official toe inspectors eliminate prospective pushers if foot cleanliness is not up to snuff. Barefoot wrestlers lock toes and — on the command "Toes away!" — attempt to "toe-down" their opponent by forcing his or her toes across the specially constructed ring, known as a "toe-rack." The tip-top toe-curler takes the best of three matches.

The **MOST TOE WRESTLING WORLD CHAMPIONSHIP WINS** title for men belongs to five-time champion Alan "Nasty" Nash of England. Alan won in 1994, 1996, 1997, 2000, and 2002. Karen Davies, also of England, holds the women's title as a four-time champion between 1999 and 2002.

MOST CONSECUTIVE DAYS SPENT SURFING

A streak of perfect waves on September 2, 1975, proved an irresistible invitation to a young surfer named Dale Webster, freshly relocated from San Diego to Valley Ford, California. His 14-day surfing paradise extended into a 28-year mission of catching at least three waves to shore every day. Hurricane winds, sharks, car problems, and kidney stones failed to interrupt Dale's daily regimen. During the years of kicking out and rolling through the mighty ocean, he married, raised a family, held several jobs, went through 30 boards and 28 wet suits, inspired generations of riders, and developed a wastewater conservation method for the redwood groves of California. On February 29, 2004, Dale retired the record for **MOST CONSECUTIVE DAYS SPENT SURFING** after enjoying 10,407 days among the waves.

TRIVIA TIDBITS
Dale's quest changed the wet suit repair warranty to 1 year *or* 10,000 waves.

MOST ENTRANTS AT A BOG SNORKELING WORLD CHAMPIONSHIP

Peat bogs are areas of wet, marshy ground filled with decaying plant matter. These swamps are plentiful in England, as is the popular sport of racing through its murky waters on foot, bike, and flipper. For the past 20 years, international competitors have submerged into the Waen Rhydd peat bog located near the small town of Llanwrtyd Wells, UK. Wearing snorkels, flippers, and wet suits, 146 people completed 2 lengths of a 60-yard trench without using any conventional swimming strokes on August 30, 2004. This turnout marked the **MOST ENTRANTS AT A BOG SNORKELING WORLD CHAMPIONSHIP**. Serious bog snorkelers can now also enter the annual mountain bike and triathlon competitions.

DID YOU KNOW?
The **MOST CONSECUTIVE BOG SNORKELING WORLD CHAMPIONSHIPS** won are three times by two competitors: Philip John (2002–2004) and Steve Griffiths (1985–1987) both of the UK.

GREATEST DEPTH BICYCLED UNDERWATER

Mountain Bike Bog Snorkeling Champions better watch out! Vittorio Innocente of Milan, Italy, combined his beloved sports of bicycling and scuba diving for a unique record-setting experience. Vittorio dove — and drove — 172.2 feet off the coast of Genoa, Italy, on July 23, 2002, on his mountain bike, dubbed *Nautilus*. The bike was modified to stay under longer by adding lead weights, flooding the tires, and fitting a plastic wing behind the seat. This trip registered as the **GREATEST DEPTH BICYCLED UNDERWATER...**

...Until Vittorio broke his own record on July 13, 2005. Determined to prove that mountain bikes really could be ridden anywhere, the 59-year-old man was lowered into the ocean off Genoa again to ride through the sea mud for a total 196.85 feet in 45 minutes.

MOST X GAMES MEDALS WON BY AN INDIVIDUAL

When he was a kid living in Chittenango, New York, Dave Mirra and friends freestyled and jumped off curbs and wooden ramps with sturdy BMX bikes. Dave started competing at bike stunt shows — and winning — at age thirteen. In 1992, "Miracle Boy" turned stunt bike riding from a hobby into a moneymaking career.

The X Games transformed a fringe sport dominated by teenagers into an ESPN-televised, international sports forum with its influence heavily felt in the Olympic categories. Dave has earned 20 X Games medals in BMX Freestyle, becoming the record-holder for **MOST X GAMES MEDALS WON BY AN INDIVIDUAL**. Of those medals, a whopping 14 are gold, doubling Dave's record tally with the **MOST X GAMES GOLD MEDALS WON BY AN INDIVIDUAL**.

DID YOU KNOW?
In January 2001, Dave caught huge air and the record for **HIGHEST BMX VERTICAL AIR** in San Diego, California. His jump off an 18-foot ramp achieved 19 feet!

HIGHEST SKYDIVING DOG

Dogs are certainly man's best friend when leaping out of a plane thousands of feet in the air! Ron Sirull brought along his canine companion, a miniature dachshund named Brutus, on his skydiving trips because it was more dangerous to leave the dog behind. Otherwise, the little dog would chase the plane down the runway.

On May 20, 1997, the **HIGHEST SKYDIVING DOG** completed his first jump at 15,000 feet above Lake Elsinore, California. By 2001, Brutus had worn his chute and custom-made goggles for a grand total of 71 dives. He has been featured in countless magazine, newspaper, and television reports. In addition to sailing among the clouds, Brutus enjoys chasing squirrels from Ron's bicycle seat and cruising the Caymans in a minisubmarine. Extreme canine sports have replaced a simple walk around the block!

MOST TENNIS BALLS HELD IN THE MOUTH BY A DOG

A golden retriever named Augie fetched prizes and a spot in the record books with his natural canine ability. The Miller family from Dallas, Texas, noticed Augie loved to fetch and hold on to tennis balls when he was a mere pup. When he was age five, they entered him in Purina's Beggin'® Strips "Stupid Dog Tricks" contest at the Grapevine Mills shopping mall. He won the local and national competitions, leading to a meeting with Guinness World Records. Augie is the certified record-holder for **MOST TENNIS BALLS HELD IN THE MOUTH BY A DOG** after he successfully gathered and held all 5 regulation-size tennis balls — without any assistance from humans — on July 6, 2003.

TRIVIA TIDBITS
Augie demonstrated his talent on *The Late Show with David Letterman*.

DID YOU KNOW?
The golden retriever is a dog breed naturally gifted in the ability to track and fetch objects.

LARGEST SIMULTANEOUS MOTORCYCLE BURNOUT

There are lots of tricks in a motorcycle rider's repertoire. A well-known trick is a "burnout." The motorcycle remains stationary while its rear wheel spins, creating smoke by burning the rubber on its tire tread.

The primary rule is to prevent injuring yourself and your bike. Mass participation events rely on each rider's cooperation and plenty of organization to get everybody doing the same thing at the same time. A total of 106 motorcycles participated in a simultaneous burnout at the Werner Rennen 2004 event at EuroSpeedway, Lausitz, Germany, on September 5, 2004.

Quiz Me!

Test your _Extreme!_ know-how with these cool quiz questions!

Q. #1
Rob Williams sure can make a sandwich fast . . . with his feet. But who is widely credited with inventing the sandwich?
a) Monsieur Mangetout
b) John Montagu, 4th Earl of Sandwich
c) Brenda Murray, 1st Empress of Eire
d) Chris Hardin, 3rd Count of Kings County

Q. #2
True or False? Toe wrestling has become so popular that it is now an Olympic event.

Q. #3
Dale Webster has been surfing every day for 28 years in California, but where did surfing originate?

Q. #4
The Bog Snorkeling World Championship is held in the British town Llanwrtyd Wells. What else is Llanwrtyd Wells' claim to fame?

Q. #5
Vittorio Innocente set a record for the **Greatest Depth Bicycled Underwater.** What do you call bicycles that can bike _on_ water?

Q. #6
True or False? Dave Mirra earned 20 medals at the X Games doing bike stunts.

Q. #7
"Para pups" were used during World War II to help the military, but could these para pups win medals for their bravery?

Q. #8
The golden retriever Augie has held five tennis balls in his mouth. What else is true about golden retrievers?
a) They are famous for their outstanding scenting abilities and can be trained to carry out search and rescue work.
b) They are great family dogs because of their tolerance of children.
c) Their calm, affectionate temperaments make them wonderful guide dogs for the blind.
d) All of the above

Q. #9
A well-known motorcycling trick is the "burnout," but which of the following are also motorcycling tricks?
a) A "Flamingo"
b) An "Endo"
c) A "Wheelie"
d) All of the above

EXTREME

KILLERS

We use our five senses of sight, sound, smell, taste, and touch to avoid danger, especially from other animals. The use of common sense is the best defense against these **LETHAL RECORD-HOLDERS.**

MOST DANGEROUS PINNIPED

Seals, sea lions, and walruses are pinnipeds, an aquatic suborder of meat-eating, flippered marine animals. The Antarctic-dwelling leopard seal (*Hydrurga leptonyx*) averages 10 feet in length, weighs up to 750 pounds, and pounces upon its prey of penguins, fish, squid, and krill. Ever wondered how an animal earns its name? The leopard seal's name originated from its skin's spotted neck area. Its reputation of ferocity came from documented reports of unprovoked attacks upon divers, including one report of a seal's aggressive pursuit of a fleeing human lasting 330 feet across the ice. Scientists think the seals may confuse a person's dark vertical shape with that of an emperor penguin. Beware, explorers! Leopard seals rightfully earned the record for **MOST DANGEROUS PINNIPED**.

MOST VENOMOUS JELLYFISH

The sea wasp is not a bug, but it can sting you! Discovered in 1955 off the coast of Queensland, the sea wasp, known in Australia as the box jellyfish (*Chironex fleckeri*), has up to 60 tentacles. Each arm contains millions of poisonous nematocysts (small external stinging cells). One box jellyfish stores enough poison to kill 60 humans. This transparent umbrella bobs along the currents or sleeps on the ocean floor. . . until a swimmer gets too close. Chemicals on our skin activate the jellyfish's nematocysts. People have died within 4 minutes after a "bite" by the **MOST VENOMOUS JELLYFISH**. This extreme killer is responsible for at least one death a year.

TRIVIA TIDBITS
You can use acetic acid, found in vinegar and human urine, to temporarily take the sting out of a jellyfish's bite before seeking immediate medical attention.

Naturalist-physician Hugo Flecker discovered a new species when local police netted the killer of several swimmers in January 1955: the box jellyfish.

KILLER RANKINGS

Watch out for these deadly record-holders! Scientists tested the natural toxins in these animals' bites, stings, and skins to determine the "lethal dose" to a mouse. (Lethal dose, or LD50, is measured in milligrams of poison necessary to kill 50% of the test subjects.)

1. **Blue-ringed Octopus 0.008 mg**
   MOST VENOMOUS MOLLUSK

2. **Puffer Fish 0.008 mg**
   MOST POISONOUS EDIBLE FISH

3. **Brazilian Huntsman Spider 0.01 mg**
   MOST VENOMOUS SPIDER

4. **Small-scaled Snake 0.025 mg**
   MOST VENOMOUS LAND SNAKE

5. **Poison Dart Frog 0.05 mg**
   MOST DANGEROUS FROG

6. **Saw-scaled Viper Snake 0.151 mg**
   SNAKE RESPONSIBLE FOR
   MOST HUMAN DEATHS

7. **Tunisian fat-tailed Scorpion 0.32 mg**
   MOST VENOMOUS SCORPION

8. **King Cobra Snake 0.35 mg**
   LONGEST VENOMOUS SNAKE

MOST VENOMOUS LAND SNAKE

Can you guess where the **MOST VENOMOUS LAND SNAKE** lives? Australia seems to be the preferred locale for several toxic species, including the small-scaled snake (*Oxyuranus microlepidotus*). The small-scaled snake prefers slithering around the Diamantina River and Cooper Creek drainage basins in Queensland and western New South Wales, Australia. These intelligent and human-shy reptiles control the rodent population by eating rats and mice. One single strike paralyzes its small prey with a mere 0.002 ounces of venom. This amount is also sufficient to kill several human adults.

When "milked," the average venom yield is 0.00155 ounces from an average specimen measuring 5 feet 7 inches long. Yet one record-breaking male yielded enough potent venom to kill 15 humans or 250,000 mice with only 0.00385 ounces! Fortunately, no human death has been reported from this snake's bite.

MOST DANGEROUS LIZARD

We leave the treacherous land of Australia to find the **MOST DANGEROUS LIZARD** in America. The Gila monster (*Heloderma suspectum*) is a brightly colored and generally harmless lizard, measuring up to 2 feet long. It takes its time crossing over arid parts of Mexico and the southwestern USA. Tough and colored scales cover a large head, short legs, stout body, and thick tail. The Gila monster is a reptilian tank, housing a powerful weapon. Eight glands in its lower jaws store enough venom to kill two adults. Unlike its cousin the snake, this reptile does not inject poison. The Gila monster chews upon its victim's skin with its needlelike, fragile teeth. If it bites deeply enough, the venom stored in its lower jaws will seep into the bite wound and infect the victim.

TRIVIA TIDBITS

Beadlike scales create the Gila monster's unusual marbled skin. Its color combinations vary between mix-and-match brown or black with orange, pink, yellow, or dull white.

DID YOU KNOW?

The name "Gila monster" refers to the Gila River Basin in Arizona.

TRIVIA TIDBITS
There are three species of cassowary (family Casuariidae), and all of them are dangerous when wounded or cornered.

MOST DANGEROUS BIRD

The **MOST DANGEROUS BIRD** lives in New Guinea and northeastern Queensland, Australia. The cassowary bird has dark feathers — except around its wattle, the brightly colored neck area. Each foot has three forward-pointing toes with claws strong enough to grip the ground while running. This bird's not-so-secret weapon is a massive 5-inch-long attack spike on each foot. The cassowary is taller than the average person at 6 feet 6 inches. If you're looking this bird in its penetrating eyes, then you're in trouble. The cassowary is nature's ultimate kickboxer. When threatened, the cassowary leaps into the air and kicks. The attack spike's sharpness, combined with a powerful kick, can rip open a person's stomach or cause enough massive blood loss to kill.

MOST VENOMOUS SPIDER

There's not just one creepy crawler killer to avoid, but a species of **MOST VENOMOUS SPIDER**. Its homeland is South America, but the Brazilian wandering spider (*Phoneutria*) loves to travel. Specimens have hitched rides in bunches of bananas on cargo ships sailing overseas! At 6.75 inches, this large, dark-colored arachnid loves nesting inside clothing, blankets, and shoes. If disturbed from its nap, it wakes up cranky and looking to bite the intruder. The amount of its venom injections varies, but hundreds of people report accidental bites every year.

The serious relative of this five-member species is the Brazilian huntsman spider (*Phoneutria fera*). It creates the most active neurotoxin of any living spider. Only 0.00000021 ounces of the huntsman's venom is potent enough to kill a mouse.

MOST DANGEROUS ANT

The bulldog ant (*Myrmecia pyriformis*) found through-out Australia is the largest of its species at .07 inches in length. This primitive and aggressive ant is unafraid of humans. Its strong jaws and tenacious grip resemble its canine namesake. Once this ant bites down, it won't let go. But its sting is worse than its bite! The bulldog ant hangs on to a victim with its long-toothed mandibles, curls its body underneath, and thrusts its long, barbless stinger into the skin repeatedly, injecting more venom each time. Adult humans allergic to such types of venom have died within 15 minutes of an attack by the **MOST DANGEROUS ANT**.

Quiz Me!

Test your *Extreme!* know-how with these cool quiz questions!

Q. #10
A leopard seal is the **Most Dangerous Pinniped**. How many documented cases have occurred of this seal species actually killing a human?

Q. #11
True or False? Jellyfish called sea wasps inject their victims with a poison that is deadlier than any snake venom.

Q. #12
The small-scaled snake is the **Most Venomous Land Snake**. Are the majority of snakes poisonous?

Q. #13
The Gila lizard is dangerous due to its venom-filled bite. How many poisonous lizards are there in the whole world?
a) 2
b) 25
c) 250
d) 2,500

Q. #14
When threatened, the cassowary bird is quite dangerous. Which of the following is also true about the cassowary?
a) It is very aggressive.
b) It can fly.
c) Meat is the mainstay of its diet.
d) None of the above

Q. #15
The **Most Dangerous Ant** is the bulldog ant species. How many species of ants are there in the whole world?
a) 10
b) 100
c) 1,000
d) More than 10,000

Q. #16
True or False? The Brazilian wandering spider has been found as far away from Brazil as Britain.

EXTREME

DANGER

The nature of record-breaking is to push beyond the established limits — those set by the previous record-holder and even your own. However, nature is full of unpredictable elements that exceed our body's limitations. Extreme danger calls for extreme **CAUTION!**

MOST DANGEROUS LOVE LIFE

In the previous chapter, we learned several hazardous creatures come from Australia. This is also the homeland of the mammal with the **MOST DANGEROUS LOVE LIFE** — and the danger comes not from other predators, but from other lovestruck males!

Every August is breeding season for the brown antechinus (*Antechinus stuartii*), a small marsupial mouse related to the Tasmanian devil. The entire adult male population spins out of control for two weeks in searching for not "one true love," but as many future mates as possible. Their quest for romance is more important than eating, sleeping, or surviving skirmishes against rival males. At the end of the season, almost all of the males have died from starvation, infection, and ulcers caused by their stressful love life. The females, however, live on to raise the young and find love again next year.

30

MOST POISONOUS EDIBLE FISH

The puffer fish (*Tetraodon*) of the Red Sea and Indo-Pacific region inhales water or air and "puffs up" to frighten predators, resembling an underwater porcupine with its scary-looking quills. The pointy skin isn't the only part of this fish that shouldn't be touched. The **MOST POISONOUS EDIBLE FISH** carries the fatal poison tetrodotoxin in its ovaries, eggs, blood, skin, liver, and intestines. Ingesting less than 0.004 ounces of this poison is fatal!

We know an untreated snakebite or serious burn may kill us, but a fish dinner? The delicate and dangerous Japanese dish named *fugu-sashi* (blowfish-raw) requires a highly trained and licensed chef in its preparation to ensure the diner's safe consumption. Improper slicing and dicing will cause the worst indigestion imaginable — the diner dies within 20 minutes of cleaning his plate!

DID YOU KNOW?

Tetrodotoxin is one of the most powerful nonproteinous poisons and 1,200 times deadlier than cyanide.

TRIVIA TIDBITS

The **MOST VENOMOUS MOLLUSK** is the blue-ringed octopus, which also carries tetrodotoxin.

SHARING A BATHTUB WITH THE MOST RATTLESNAKES

Known as "The Texas Snake Man," Jackie Bibby counts snakes among his closest friends. He should, having been trained in the professional art of snake handling since high school. Jackie has worn coiled rattlers upon his head in place of his trademark bowler; dangled 8 by their tails from his mouth (one record); crawled willingly into a sleeping bag packed with 109 not-so-sleepy reptiles (a second record); and lounged in a bathtub filled with 75 live western diamondback rattlesnakes (a third record). Bibby shared the latter record-making experience of **SHARING A BATHTUB WITH THE MOST RATTLE-SNAKES** with coholder Rosie Reynolds-McCasland on September 24, 1999. Jackie and Rosie sat in two separate, equally snake-filled bathtubs placed alongside each other on the set of *Guinness World Records: Primetime* in Los Angeles, California.

LONGEST DURATION OF FIRE TORCH TEETHING

Any action involving the unpredictable element of fire requires taking lots of precautions. . . and having a quick way of dousing flames at the ready. Breathing fire is extremely dangerous for the performer and audience. Improper inhalation or exhalation can cause a "blow back," scorching the breather's lungs or burning an onlooker. This trick falls under the category of "Do Not Try This at Home!" Serious training is required for jugglers, circus performers, and magicians who learn how to manipulate special torches, fuel, and breathing techniques.

Matthew J. Cassiere adopted the stage name of "Matt the Knife" (MTK) when he became a professional performance artist, consultant, writer, and multiple record-breaker in several hazardous categories. On October 30, 2004, MTK held a lit torch vertically in his teeth for 23 seconds. This act reset the record in **LONGEST DURATION FOR FIRE TORCH TEETHING**.

TRIVIA TIDBITS
Matt the Knife is a member of the International Brotherhood of Magicians.

DID YOU KNOW?
Matt the Knife currently holds 2 additional Guinness World Records: **FASTEST HANDCUFF ESCAPE**, and **FASTEST UNDERWATER HANDCUFF ESCAPE**.

MOST VIRULENT VIRAL DISEASE

Ebola hemorrhagic fever causes death in up to 90 percent of its victims. While the exact origin of the disease is unknown, cases have been seen in humans since the 1970s throughout Africa. Recognition of the disease and its virulent cause occurred in 1976 when 318 people from the Democratic Republic of the Congo (formerly Zaire) became infected. Scientists hypothesize that transmission of the Ebola virus begins with an animal to a human. Patients suffer high fevers and bleeding from eyes, ears, and nose. These secretions are highly contagious and the reason for the swiftness of outbreaks among family members and health-care workers. Although there is no cure yet, the disease is extremely rare, with less than 1,200 reported deaths since its 1976 discovery. The animal source will need to be identified before transmission can be contained and a cure is developed for the **MOST VIRULENT VIRAL DISEASE.**

TRIVIA TIDBITS
Three of the four identified subtypes of the Ebola virus have caused disease in humans.

DEADLIEST LAKE

On the night of August 21, 1986, a massive amount of carbon dioxide (CO_2) burst from Lake Nyos in Cameroon, West Africa. A poisonous cloud formed over the immediate area, depriving thousands of animals and 1,746 people of oxygen. Survivors far enough outside of the lake's vicinity recall only falling asleep while others suffocated to death.

When scientists investigated the tragedy, they discovered several factors contributing to create a lethal combination. Lake Nyos lies in a dormant volcano crater. Perhaps the gas was volcanic in nature. Water in most lakes naturally mixes as seasons change. Tropical lakes feature steady temperatures and the water forms layers, with a lack of circulation thereby trapping any gases beneath decomposing plant materials on the lake surface. Although the gases' origins are debated, the deadly results are not. The gas lay trapped at the bottom of Lake Nyos and had enough time to turn toxic before its release on that fateful night.

Since this tragedy, scientists have been "burping" the **DEADLIEST LAKE** — forcing out the built-up gas at regulated times and tolerable levels.

Quiz Me!

Test your *Extreme!* know-how with these cool quiz questions!

Q. #17
The brown antechinus is a mammal that is noted for having the **Most Dangerous Love Life**. What *spider* is well known for its deadly mating habits?

Q. #18
Are the Japanese aware of how dangerous it is to eat the poisonous puffer fish called *fugu-sashi*?

Q. #19
Jackie Bibby has shared quite a lot of time with rattlesnakes, but do rattlesnakes always rattle before they strike?

Q. #20
Matt the Knife is a member of what "magical organization"?

Q. #21
True or False? Carbon dioxide is heavier than air.

Q. #22
The Ebola virus is the most dangerous in the world. How many cases have been reported in the US?
a) 12
b) 2
c) 1
d) 0

EXTREME

SPEED

The human **NEED TO MOVE FASTER** than our rivals began as a survival trait. Today, we can zoom through life on foot, wing, and lawn mower, taking record-breaking to new speeds!

WINNER

FARTHEST DISTANCE COVERED IN A LAWN MOWER RACE

When asked to mow the lawn, don't look at it as a boring chore. . . it's training for future glory at the lawn mower racing championships! This cutting-edge sport got its grassroots start in Britain, as a money-saving alternative to the mounting expenses of racing cars. Everyone had a lawn mower and a different style of pushing, riding, or steering. The speed limit averaged, at the time, a meager 35 miles per hour. (Today's riders hit 83 mph on modified machines.)

On a hazy August afternoon in 1973, the newly formed British Lawn Mower Racing Association held the first annual 12-hour world championship. Blades were removed, automatic-shutoff switches enabled, and protective gear required to pass safety inspections. Since then, the sport has sprouted into international competitions and all-ages popularity. The **FARTHEST DISTANCE COVERED IN A LAWN MOWER RACE** was 313.6 miles at Wisborough Green, UK, during the 25th annual world championship on August 29–30, 1998. Ian Dobson, Robert Jones, and Steve Williams (all UK) of the team "Extreme Headless Chickens" mowed down the competition for the record.

FASTEST FURNITURE

Couch potatoes, rejoice! You don't have to leave your comfy sofa behind to run errands, but you might have to relocate to Britain. Edd China and David Davenport (both from the UK) design and build furniture-on-the-go. Using a variety of base vehicles, these machine modifiers create speedy bathtubs, toilets, four-poster beds, and a fur-covered car. The **FASTEST FURNITURE** is a motorized sofa. The fully licensed "Casual Lofa" rumbles along UK roads at 87 mph. Its mileage reads 6,210 miles traveled since March 1998.

The speedy sofa is powered by a Mini 1300-cc engine and steered by a medium-size pizza pan (complete with a pepperoni pizza for snacking). Two passengers can lounge while the driver uses a chocolate bar to hand-shift between the sofa's four automatic gears and a cola can for a braking system. Signal lights are housed beneath two flowerpots. The front bumper coffee table supports a clock, a TV, and the speedometer.

TRIVIA TIDBITS
The knee throttle gives the driver a choice of a feet-up or feet-down driving position.

DID YOU KNOW?
A black-and-white television provides the in-car entertainment.

AND THE WINNER IS...

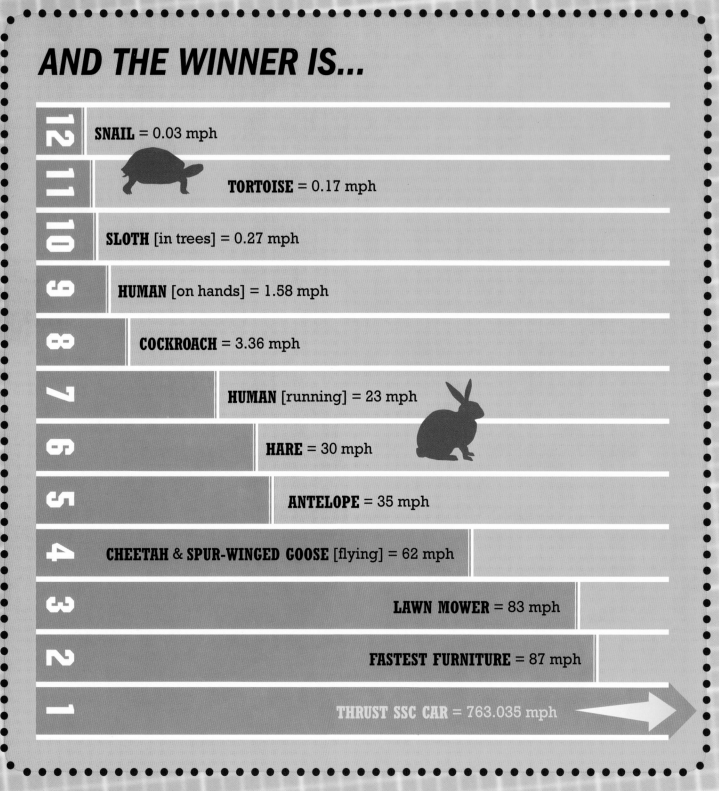

12 — **SNAIL** = 0.03 mph

11 — **TORTOISE** = 0.17 mph

10 — **SLOTH** [in trees] = 0.27 mph

9 — **HUMAN** [on hands] = 1.58 mph

8 — **COCKROACH** = 3.36 mph

7 — **HUMAN** [running] = 23 mph

6 — **HARE** = 30 mph

5 — **ANTELOPE** = 35 mph

4 — **CHEETAH & SPUR-WINGED GOOSE** [flying] = 62 mph

3 — **LAWN MOWER** = 83 mph

2 — **FASTEST FURNITURE** = 87 mph

1 — **THRUST SSC CAR** = 763.035 mph

FASTEST MAN AND WOMAN

The first edition of *Guinness World Records* in 1955 recognized six coholders for **FASTEST MAN — 100 M**. The 100-meter dash was the measuring distance for this claim and all six men had achieved 10.2 seconds as hand-timed by stop-watches, although the years and countries varied.

Times, literally, changed to electronic measurements in splitting one second into hundredths of a second. On June 14, 2005, Asafa Powell crossed the finish line of the 100-meter dash in a blistering, record-setting 9.77 seconds. Currently, Asafa is the **FASTEST MAN — 100 M**. The companion record for **FASTEST WOMAN — 100 M** remains with Florence Griffith Joyner, who blazed through the 100-meter dash in 10.49 seconds on July 16, 1988. Her death in 1998 at the age of 38 did not diminish her record status as, to date, her performance remains unequaled.

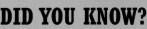

FASTEST WINGBEAT OF AN INSECT

The tiny midge of the genus *Forcipomyia* is microscopic in size, earning its nickname of "no-see-um"... until it bites you. As larvae, these algae-eating flies inhabit watery areas around the globe. The adults move into moist, ground-based areas, such as rotting wood, tree holes, and salt marshes. Scientists tested the speed of various bugs' wingbeats and crowned the tiny midge with the title of **FASTEST WINGBEAT OF AN INSECT** for its incredible 62,760 beats per minute, achieved under natural conditions. The muscular contraction-expansion cycle of 0.00045 seconds required for such rapid wingbeats is currently the fastest muscle movement ever measured.

DID YOU KNOW?

People owe the tiny midge fly a big thank-you. This insect is the only pollinator of the cacao tree, the source of chocolate-producing cacao beans!

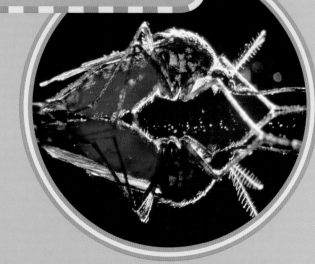

FASTEST-MOVING INSECT

People can create a sport out of *anything*. As we've seen in this chapter, all you need is a speedy object, a working stopwatch, and a crowd of cheering spectators.

The legendary pastime among Russian czars was bug racing... specifically cockroaches, a long-lived species with about 4,000 different types scuttling around the world. In 1991, the University of California in Berkeley, California, scientifically proved what many racing enthusiasts already knew. The **FASTEST-MOVING INSECT** record belongs to *Periplaneta americana*, a large tropical cockroach of the order Dictyoptera. The insect was clocked at 3.36 miles per hour. That works out to moving 50 body lengths per second!

TRIVIA TIDBITS

Brisbane, Australia, is home to more than 450 cockroach species. The city hosted its 23rd annual Cockroach Races in January 2005. Over 7,000 attendees participated in the charity event for a local children's hospital.

Quiz Me!

Test your *Extreme!* know-how with these cool quiz questions!

Q. #23
True or False? The largest irrigated crop in the United States is grass.

Q. #24
Edd China and David Davenport built a speedy sofa, traveling 87 mph. But which of the following pieces of furniture is designed to always be "on-the-go"?
a) Cupboard
b) The Murphy Bed
c) Love seat
d) None of the above

Q. #25
How many Olympic medals has Asafa Powell, currently the **Fastest Man – 100 M**, won?

Q. #26
We know the midge can sure "shake a wing," but which of the following is also true about the midge?
a) It looks like a tiny mosquito.
b) Its larvae resemble worms.
c) It can be found on every continent.
d) All of the above

Q. #27
A cockroach is the **Fastest-Moving Insect**. Which of the following also shows the cockroach's amazing survival tactics?
a) It can live without a head for up to a week.
b) It will eat anything — including another cockroach!
c) It can live for a month without food.
d) All of the above

EXTREME ON

THE MOVE

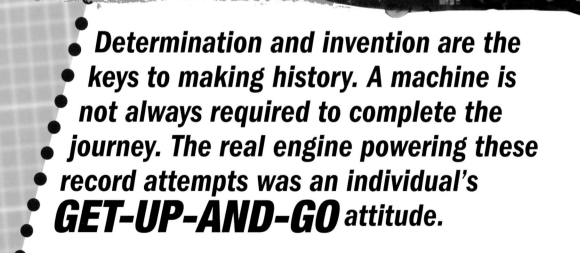

Determination and invention are the keys to making history. A machine is not always required to complete the journey. The real engine powering these record attempts was an individual's **GET-UP-AND-GO** attitude.

FASTEST LAND SPEED

Land speed record attempts began in 1898 when Count Gaston de Chasseloup-Laubat of France finished a single run through a course. His average speed was 39.24 mph.

Almost 100 years later, Andy Green broke his own previous record for **FASTEST LAND SPEED** — and the sound barrier — in the seat of Thrust SSC. The supersonic car was powered by two Rolls-Royce Spey 202 jet engines, generating 50,000 pounds of thrust.

The Thrust car series consisted of three different vehicles, with the second and third cars driven to various land speed records through the years by the team of Green and Richard Noble. The first land speed record of 633.47 mph, set by Richard in Thrust 2, came and went on October 4, 1983. Andy took the third car, Thrust SSC, past Richard's mark at 714.10 mph on September 25, 1997.

A few days later, Andy climbed behind the wheel again on October 15, 1997. When Thrust SSC tore through the Black Rock Desert in Nevada at 763.035 mph, or Mach 1.02, the car created a shock wave in front of it and broke through the sound barrier with a massive sonic boom.

TRIVIA TIDBITS
Andy Green was a Royal Air Force fighter pilot before he broke the sound barrier behind the wheel of a car.

DID YOU KNOW?
Reaching the limit in land speed and sound barrier records will depend upon the human body's ability to withstand the gravitational pressure, or G-forces, of acceleration.

The Fédération Internationale de l'Automobile (FIA) governs motor sport worldwide and officiates every land speed record attempt.

FASTEST CROSSING OF THE ENGLISH CHANNEL BY AMPHIBIOUS VEHICLE

The journey doesn't have to stop where the road ends and the water begins. . . if you're driving an amphibious vehicle. The blending of sports car and speedboat mechanics dates back to 1899 in Denmark. Today, Gibbs Technologies of the UK offers the Aquada for road-and-water enthusiasts. The doorless hull has been tested to withstand leaks and saltwater corrosion. The vehicle reaches 100 miles per hour on the road and 35 miles per hour on water. The 12-second transformation from car to boat occurs at the press of a button. Wheels retract, and the engine cues a jet to expel 1 ton of thrust, the amount of force required for a vehicle to skim across the water.

The record for the **FASTEST CROSSING OF THE ENGLISH CHANNEL BY AMPHIBIOUS VEHICLE** is 43 minutes and 12 seconds, achieved by Maurice Bryham (NZ) co-piloted by Nick Fox and Hugo Andreae (both UK) to Sangatte, France on June 21, 2005 in a vehicle called Sealegs.

DID YOU KNOW?
Sealegs can travel at speeds up to 37 miles per hour on water, but only 9.3 miles per hour on land.

DEEPEST DIVING SUBMERSIBLE IN SERVICE

The Japanese research submarine *Shinkai 6500* is the **DEEPEST DIVING SUBMERSIBLE IN SERVICE**. The craft's name refers to its maximum depth limitation of 6,500 meters. On August 11, 1989, the vessel surpassed its own limits by 27 meters for a depth of 21,414 feet in the Japan Trench off Sanriku, Japan. The 3-person craft (2 pilots and 1 researcher) is 31 feet long, 8 feet 10 inches wide, and 10 feet 6 inches high. The sub is launched from a research vessel, such as *Yokosuka*. The craft is capable of submerging for up to 8 hours. Its mission is to collect samples, install observation instruments on the seafloor, and capture video and still footage underwater. The *Shinkai 6500* is a valuable tool in sea research and the continued study of geophysics, geology, and earthquake prediction. Currently, it is continuing its exploration of the world's seabed.

TRIVIA TIDBITS
JAMSTEC's (Japan Marine Science and Technology Center) unmanned second submersible, *Kaiko*, verified the **DEEPEST POINT IN THE OCEAN** with a test dive of 35,797 feet into the Pacific Ocean's Mariana Trench in March 1995.

LONGEST DISTANCE WALKING ON HANDS

Some people like to walk the road less traveled. And then there's Johann Hurlinger, the record-holder for **LONGEST DISTANCE WALKING ON HANDS**. An Austrian man living in the early 1900s, Johann decided to give his feet a rest and let his fingers do the walking . . . or more precisely, his palms and wrists. For 10 hours each day, his hands walked from Vienna, Austria, to Paris, France. He averaged 1.58 miles per hour. The total distance covered in those grueling 55 days was a muscle-aching 870 miles. Now there's an example of repetitive stress injury!

Johann's record has not been broken for a century. Those interested should have strong arms, tough palms, a good sense of balance, and an idea of where they're headed since they'll be keeping their eyes on the road.

> **TRIVIA TIDBITS**
> At home in France, Rémy Bricka plays 24 instruments strapped to his body and is called "L'homme Orchestre," or the "One-Man Band."

> **DID YOU KNOW?**
> Gymnasts advise would-be record-breakers to master the handstand *first*. From there, you can take your first steps. It's just like walking. . . but upside down.

FASTEST ATLANTIC CROSSING WALK ON WATER

Frenchman Rémy Bricka first crossed the Atlantic Ocean aboard a steamship. It was 1972, and Rémy decided his next crossing would be as captain of his own fate, not a passenger along for the ride.

His next crossing of the Atlantic Ocean began on April 2, 1988. Determined to "walk," Rémy fit his feet inside polyester ski floats, dragged a floating pod carrying few supplies behind him, and steered with a double-headed paddle. His departure dock was Tenerife in the Spanish Canary Islands. Rémy covered 3,502 miles, eating plankton on the way, before a Japanese trawler helped him dock in Trinidad on May 31, 1988. Rémy's determination and extraordinary two-month journey registered as the **FASTEST ATLANTIC CROSSING WALK ON WATER**.

LARGEST LAND TRANSPORT VEHICLE

The 6-million-pound (2,721-ton) crawler-transporter slowly moving through Florida's Kennedy Space Center is the **LARGEST LAND TRANSPORT VEHICLE** used for moving objects between two points. Two of these mechanical behemoths have been in operation since 1967, charged with the critical — and backbreaking — task of transporting space shuttles to and from their launch pads. Although these are *not* the **LARGEST MOBILE MACHINES**, the crawler's individual size and operating capacity are record-setting statistics. Each machine is 20 feet high, 131 feet wide, 114 feet long, and runs on 8 giant tank-style tracks. The family car may get a flat tire, but these crawlers need a new 2,000-pound "shoe" if a track becomes worn.

A mission starts when the crawler picks up its load from the vehicle assembly building. This is a fully assembled space shuttle, mounted on a mobile launcher platform, and weighing another 6 million pounds! A loaded crawler averages a speed of 1 mile per hour on its way to the launching pad.

BIGGEST SKATEBOARD

Foundation Skateboards founder and skater Tod Swank believes life should be lived to the extreme — in a radical, alternative, uniquely sized, revolutionary manner. So why not grab a bunch of fellow skating pals to build the **BIGGEST SKATEBOARD**? Construction on the WBS (World's Biggest Skateboard) started in 1996 in San Diego, California. Certification by Guinness World Records was achieved on October 4, 2004. Tod shares design and production credit with Greg Winter, Dana Hard, and Damon Mills. The giant board stretches 12 feet long. Riders can stand on the 4-feet-wide surface, after they boost themselves 2 feet 6 inches off the ground to get aboard. Its hot rod wheels were donated by a sports car. Its scaled-up double trucks turn when the board is tilted, just like on a regular-size skateboard. Five riders on board, working together, can surf the sidewalk without falling off. The only problem — no brakes on 500 pounds of runaway board!

TRIVIA TIDBITS

The design team's next dream: a truly gigantic skateboard about the size of a car, but this time with a fully operational braking system!

DID YOU KNOW?

The WBS is rolling through promotional stops across America, but watch out: Other skaters are trying to build an even *bigger* board!

FOUNDATION SUPER CO.

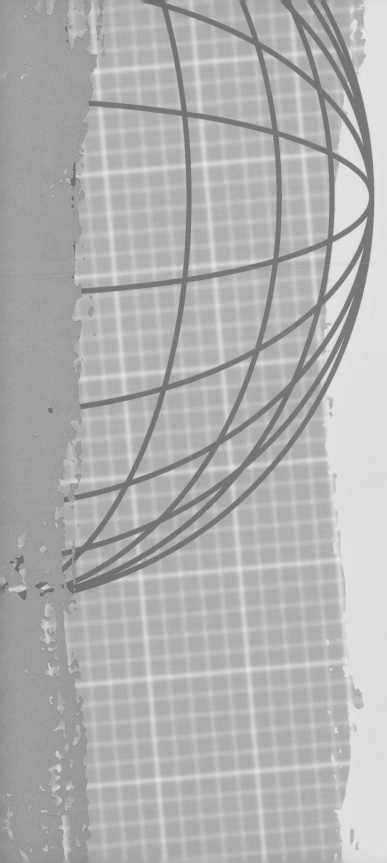

Quiz Me!

Test your *Extreme!* know-how with these cool quiz questions!

Q. #28
When Andy Green broke the sound barrier with his Thrust SSC, it caused a sonic boom. Can a sonic boom hurt you?

Q. #29
Sealegs offers a speedy way to get across the English Channel, reaching speeds of 37 mph on water. What's a more common (not to mention faster) way to cross the English Channel?

Q. #30
The *Shinkai 6500* is capable of surveying approximately what percentage of the world's oceans?
a) 12 percent
b) 98 percent
c) 66 percent
d) None of the above

Q. #31
What insect can walk on water, and without the polyester ski floats that keep Rémy Bricka afloat?

Q. #32
What do Adho Mukha Vrksasana and a normal handstand have to do with each other?

Q. #33
Since the two NASA crawler-transporters have been in use, how many miles, in total, have they traveled?

Q. #34
True or False? The first skateboard was developed in the twentieth century by surfers who made them using roller skates.

EXTREME

1914

SAL

SOUNDS

In our modern age, we race through life with a right earpiece for our phone and a left earpiece for our digitized playlists. We ask others if they can hear us **OVER THE NOISE** — while our musical world plays on around us.

53

DEEPEST NOTE IN THE UNIVERSE

The **DEEPEST NOTE IN THE UNIVERSE** is a B-flat, 57 octaves below middle C. It's the song of a dying galaxy and has been playing for about 2.5 billion years!

A supermassive black hole in the center of the Perseus cluster of galaxies — 250 million light-years away — generates acoustic waves through a thin layer of surrounding gases. We can't hear it, because the decibel level (dBA) is more than a million billion times lower than the human ear can detect. Professor Andrew Fabian of Cambridge University led astronomers in this discovery after 270 hours of observations at the Chandra X-ray Observatory.

LOUDEST BURP

Some maestros try to make music out of the noises made by the human body during the act of digestion. For a burp, your stomach releases gases that rise up through your esophagus and out of your mouth. Different cultures either declare this rude behavior or applaud its proper commentary on a good meal. Fizzy beverages, such as carbonated sodas, and gassy foods, such as cauliflower or broccoli, can cause big-time burps.

Paul Hunn of the United Kingdom released the **LOUDEST BURP** in the London offices of Guinness World Records on July 20, 2004. Officials measured the burp's sound from 8 feet 2 inches away, and 3 feet 3 inches high from Paul. His burp measured a whopping 104.9 decibels on a certified and calibrated class 1 precision measuring noise-level meter. Paul's bellyful was an earful: His decibel level was higher than a pile driver heard from a distance of 100 feet!

DID YOU KNOW?
Paul Hunn's secret combination for boisterous burps: fizzy soda and big gulps of air!

TRIVIA TIDBITS
Sleep apnea is very common, afflicting an estimated 12 million Americans.

LOUDEST SNORE

Snoring is a sign of respiratory problems, an annoyance, and noisy sleep disturbance, but not technically a "talent" according to Guinness World Records. However, they did recognize the extraordinary sound level of the **LOUDEST SNORE** by Kåre Walkert of Sweden. On May 24, 1993, Kåre's recorded peak snoring levels tipped the noise level meter at 93 dBA. The snore's decibel equivalent is a jackhammer breaking up concrete heard from 50 feet away! The loud outbursts are symptoms of the breathing disorder apnea from which Kåre suffers. Relaxed throat muscles, enlarged tonsils or adenoids, or a long uvula block the airway. Breathing becomes labored and louder, until the sleeper falls silent . . . unable to breathe. The brain releases adrenaline to awaken the sleeper and restore proper circulation of oxygen, blood, and carbon dioxide. Snorers, and their suffering companions, should seek out the advice of their physician. Sometimes the solution is as simple as changing sleeping positions for a real good night's sleep.

DID YOU HEAR THAT?

LOUDNESS and decibel level depend on how near your ear gets to the source of the sound. Noises below 30 dBA are often ignored, with **PAIN** experienced around 130 dBA. Noises over 160 dBA instantly perforate the eardrum and cause permanent deafness.

1. Lab-created **HORN** blown = **210 dBA** (*sound bored holes through solid material*)

2. **BLUE WHALE** = **188 dBA**

3. Woman's **SCREAM** = **129 dBA**

4. **WHISTLING** = **125 dBA**

5. Military **JET AIRCRAFT** taking off = **120 dBA**

6. Front row at a **ROCK CONCERT** = **110 dBA**

7. **SNAPPING** fingers = **108 dBA** (*and lawn mower heard from 3 feet away*)

8. African **CICADA** = **106.8 dBA**

9. **BURPING** = **104.9 dBA**

10. **SNORING** = **93 dBA** (*and jackhammer heard from 50 feet away*)

11. **CLAPPING** hands = **73 dBA**

12. **CAR** going 65 mph, heard from 25 feet away = **80 dBA**

13. **CONVERSATIONAL SPEECH** from 1 foot away = **60 dBA**

14. **BIRD CALL** = **40 dBA**

14 13 12 11 10 9 8 7 6 5 4 3 2 1

LARGEST ANIMAL ORCHESTRA WITH THE MOST MEMBERS

In 2000, Americans Richard Lair and David Soldier composed a melodious method of promoting the conservation of the endangered Asiatic elephant. The humans founded the 12-piece Thai Elephant Orchestra, also known as the **LARGEST ANIMAL ORCHESTRA WITH THE MOST MEMBERS**. The musicians' ages range between 7 and 18 years old. These music-loving pachyderms perform improvised and traditional melodies using a variety of specially designed percussion and wind instruments. Humans cue them at the piece's opening and closing, but the elephants select the notes and rhythms. David accompanies the "ellies" as lead violinist in traditional Thai tunes, plus a sampling of classics from Beethoven to Hank Williams. All types of audiences are invited to attend their concerts held at the Thai Elephant Conservation Center in Lampang, Thailand. The band doesn't tour, but their second album, *Elephant Rhapsodies*, is on sale, with a third in the works.

DID YOU KNOW?
Elephants paint! Keep your ears perked for another pachyderm pastime later on in this book.

LARGEST SIMULTANEOUS YODEL

People think yodeling is a wildly pitched song warbled only between Alpine mountain people, yet many cultures — European, African, Hawaiian, Mexican, and American — use this songlike cry in communication and entertainment.

There are solo-yodeling records for longest and loudest, with the category of **LARGEST SIMULTANEOUS YODEL** bringing in the crowds. On October 5, 2002, a group of 937 yodelers sang the popular Swiss tune, *Von Luzern uf Wäggis zue*, for more than one minute. The event took place at the Ravensburger Spieleland in Meckenbeuren, Germany.

The current record holder is Yahoo! Inc., the global Internet company based in Sunnyvale, California. The company known for its yodeling corporate theme gathered 1,795 people at its headquarters on November 19, 2004. Wylie Gustafson, the original Yahoo! yodeler, alongside the winner of the company's yodel challenge, 9-year-old Taylor Marie Ware, showed the others the proper way to yodel their way through a record attempt.

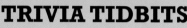

TRIVIA TIDBITS

The American style of yodeling is influenced by European and African styles. Popular singers, such as Gene Autry and Hank Williams, rapidly shifted vocal tones between normal and falsetto in their songs.

MOST DJS IN RELAY

DJs were in heavy demand and rotation at London's Bridge and Tunnel Club during a charity event and record attempt. An Internet-based music club, d-train, celebrated its first anniversary by setting the record for **MOST DJS IN RELAY**. Starting at 7:00 PM on June 18, 2003, "disc jockeys" jumped behind the decks to spin one record each, with every mix continuous, synchronous, and to professional standards for 4 hours. At least one person had to be moving and grooving on the dance floor throughout the show. A total of 59 DJs shared their eclectic range with a mash-up of beats from Afro, hip-hop, house, and drum 'n' bass. At the dropping of tune No. 51, this harmonious event broke the previous Guinness World Record spun by 50 musical hosts.

DID YOU KNOW?

DJs select and play sound recordings, but they can also manipulate the output and create original compositions through various techniques of cueing, sampling, cutting, scratching, and beat-matching.

Quiz Me!

Test your *Extreme!* know-how with these cool quiz questions!

Q. #35
True or False? A black hole is a hole.

Q. #36
True or False? British Paul Hunn sure can burp, but is it true that in some cultures burping is okay, and even polite?

Q. #37
Sleep apnea, or snoring, is quite common. Which of the following are other sleeping disorders?
a) Somnambulism
b) Narcolepsy
c) Bruxism
d) All of the above

Q. #38
The Elephant Orchestra is quite talented, but what do "Little Elephant Saddle," "Floating down the Pin River," "Pin Pia," "Bamboolin," "Dancing with Prathida," and "Kaw-Liga" have to do with them?

Q. #39
The term "DJ" refers to "disc jockey." What is a modern play on this term?

Q. #40
While yodeling can be found in many cultures, where did it start?

EXTREME

SMELLS

In our world today, a great deal of time, money, and effort is put into smelling the "right" way. These record-breaking **TOUGH ODORS & MIGHTY SNIFFERS** overwhelm the senses to leave a lasting impression.

MOST SENSITIVE NOSE FOR A LAND MAMMAL

Nature equipped the **LARGEST LAND CARNIVORE** with powerful hunting tools for survival amid the Arctic's harsh living conditions. Temperatures below -50° F don't slow down a polar bear insulated with two layers of fur and a 4.5-inch-thick layer of blubber. The hunter's tools consist of impressive size (between 6 to 10 feet tall), bulky weight (up to 1,320 pounds), sharp claws for fishing, a stomach capacity of 150 pounds, ice-proof footpads, and the **MOST SENSITIVE NOSE FOR A LAND MAMMAL**. This fierce hunter follows the faintest whiff of a possible future meal — even if its prey is 18 miles away and under thick ice. Bears have been documented walking in a straight line for 20 miles, running hundreds of miles from shore across ice, and swimming 60 miles in pursuit of a fleeing seal.

The polar bear also hunts walruses (1,100 pounds) and the world's **LARGEST PREY**, beluga whales (1,320 pounds). It should also be noted that the polar bear's digestive system, being more suited to processing meat rather than vegetation, makes it the most carnivorous of its species.

TRIVIA TIDBITS
Cubs born in early wintertime stay in the snow den until early springtime. They are born blind, toothless, and completely dependent upon their mother for warmth and food.

DID YOU KNOW?
The scientific name for the polar bear is *Ursus maritimus* or "sea bear."

MOST ACUTE SENSE OF SMELL

Bugs don't have noses like other animals, but they do have sensitive antennae and use these feelers to guide them in search of food, safety, and love! The male emperor moth (*Eudia pavonia*) rules over the bug kingdom with its impressive skill in locating its mate. This orange-hued flier, found throughout Europe and Asia, boldly flits about in daylight. Its mate, although larger in size by 2 to 3 inches, is a soft gray color and moves cautiously during nighttime. According to the results of German experiments carried out in 1961, the **MOST ACUTE SENSE OF SMELL** among the insect world belongs to the male emperor moth. Its antennae chemoreceptors can detect a female moth from 6.8 miles away with only one molecule of her pheromones.

TRIVIA TIDBITS
Anosmia is the medical term for being unable to detect or recognize any odor.

MOST FEET AND ARMPITS SNIFFED

The average human being can recognize approximately 10,000 different smells. Laboratories, such as Hill Top Research in Cincinnati, Ohio, hire olfactory testers, or professional sniffers, in the development and testing of health and personal care products. After 15 years of being an olfactory tester, Madeline Albrecht and her discerning nose broke into the record books with **MOST FEET AND ARMPITS SNIFFED**. Madeline had personally verified the effects of the lab's odor-reducing products upon approximately 5,600 feet and thousands of armpits by the year 2000. Now that's a professional hard at work!

DID YOU KNOW?
The feet have 250,000 sweat glands and excrete about half a pint of moisture every day!

SMELLIEST FLOWER

The *Amorphophallus titanum* is an impressive sight since it blooms once every 1 to 3 years, usually in the Sumatran rain forests, and lives for a brief span of a few days. Spiked, burgundy-colored petals unfurl and the tubor shoots skyward, achieving the stately heights of 6.5 feet to 11 feet. Since 1889, horticulturists have been able to cultivate this flower under controlled conditions in parts of Europe and the United States. Within a city's botanical exhibit, curious onlookers lean in for a whiff of the rare tropical flower blooming. And then everyone, except scavenger animals and flies, beats a hasty retreat for the door.

The odor released by the **SMELLIEST FLOWER** resembles decaying meat, and you can catch the scent of the "corpse flower" a half mile away! The bloom's odor and the petals' meaty color attract carrion bugs to help with pollination. Two to four days from the flower's blooming, the plant itself dies.

DID YOU KNOW?

The corpse flower also has the **LARGEST BLOOM**. On May 23, 2003, the Bonn University's Botanical Gardens cultivated a 10-foot-high sample of this dual record-holder in Bonn, Germany.

TRIVIA TIDBITS

In 1878, Italian botanist Dr. Oroardo Beccari discovered the corpse flower among the rain forests of Indonesia.

LARGEST GARLIC FESTIVAL

Rivalries among record claims exist even at a city level. In 1978, Dr. Rudy Melone, president of Gavilan College in Gilroy, California, read a news article about a tiny French village claiming to be the garlic capital of the world. He decided the world needed to taste the truth: The garlic soup in Arleux, France, might be tasty, but it wouldn't hold a candle to the fire-breathing, homegrown creation cooked up by Gilroy's chefs!

Since 1979, the last weekend in July has attracted garlic lovers numbering in the millions for the three-day, aromatic Gilroy Garlic Festival. The **LARGEST GARLIC FESTIVAL** honors this vegetable's place in the world and attracts 130,000 people each year! Garlic farming is the major business of Gilroy, and all proceeds from the festival are fed back into the community. Every festival kicks off with the lighting of a 25-foot fake bulb of garlic. Participants then sample a wide range of garlic-flavored food — everything from meat to ice cream — whipped up by enthusiastic volunteers!

Quiz Me!

Test your *Extreme!* know-how with these cool quiz questions!

Q. #41

Polar bears are huge carnivores. These hunters have sharp claws, a stomach capacity of 150 pounds, and the **Most Sensitive Nose for a Land Mammal** — but can they outrun a human on land?

Q. #42

The male emperor moth can detect a female moth from 6.8 miles away with the scent of only one molecule of her pheromones. What exactly is a pheromone?

Q. #43

"Anosmia" is the medical term for being unable to detect or recognize any odor, but what's the medical term for being able to smell?

Q. #44

True or False? The *Amorphophallus titanum*, or "corpse flower," can be as tall as a grown man.

Q. #45

We know that garlic is used in many recipes, even ice cream, and is good for you, but when did people first start eating it?

EXTREME

EXTENSIONS

Some people are born into record-making history while others make their mark with their own sense of style. You'll have to extend your ruler **A FEW MORE INCHES** for these lengthy record-breakers.

MOST FINGERS AND TOES ON A LIVING PERSON

How many times have you wished for one more finger or toe to make life easier? The condition of being born with more than the average number of 5 fingers and 5 toes on each hand and foot is called polydactylism, and occurs among animals and humans. Any one of over 30 medical syndromes present at birth can cause additional digits. Most commonly these are fleshy bumps without any bones, but occasionally they can be completely formed fingers or toes. The condition is actually relatively common, with as many as 2 in 1,000 births affected, or even higher depending on several population factors.

There have been record-holders in this category since the first publication of the original *Guinness Book of World Records*, and there will be people with even more astonishing digits in the future. Currently, the record for **MOST FINGERS AND TOES ON A LIVING PERSON** belongs to Devendra Harne of India, who has 25 in total (12 fingers and 13 toes).

DID YOU KNOW?
The word "polydactyl" has its roots in Greek, meaning "many fingers."

LONGEST NOSE ON A LIVING PERSON

In 1897, Edmond Rostand wrote a famous dramatic stage play, *Cyrano de Bergerac*, about a sensitive man challenged in life by the considerable length of his nose. In 2001, a different man, named Mehmet Ozyurek, enjoys the fuss other people make over his impressive nose.

Turkish-born Mehmet is a construction worker in his hometown of Artvin. The Black Sea region of the country is known for celebrating the size of its people's noses. There is an annual long-nose competition where both men and women line up against a ruler made of anchovy bone. Mehmet stuck out against 22 other nasally inclined rivals to be declared the proud winner. Guinness World Records used a more standard ruler to verify the measurements on January 31, 2001. Mehmet's nose, extending 3.46 inches from the bridge to the tip, was declared the **LONGEST NOSE ON A LIVING PERSON.**

TRIVIA TIDBITS
Historical accounts from the 1770s state that a circus performer named Thomas Wedders had a nose measuring 7.5 inches—the **LONGEST NOSE EVER**!

DID YOU KNOW?
Cyrano de Bergerac was a real-life French soldier and writer in the 17th century.

71

THEY GO TO GREAT LENGTHS!

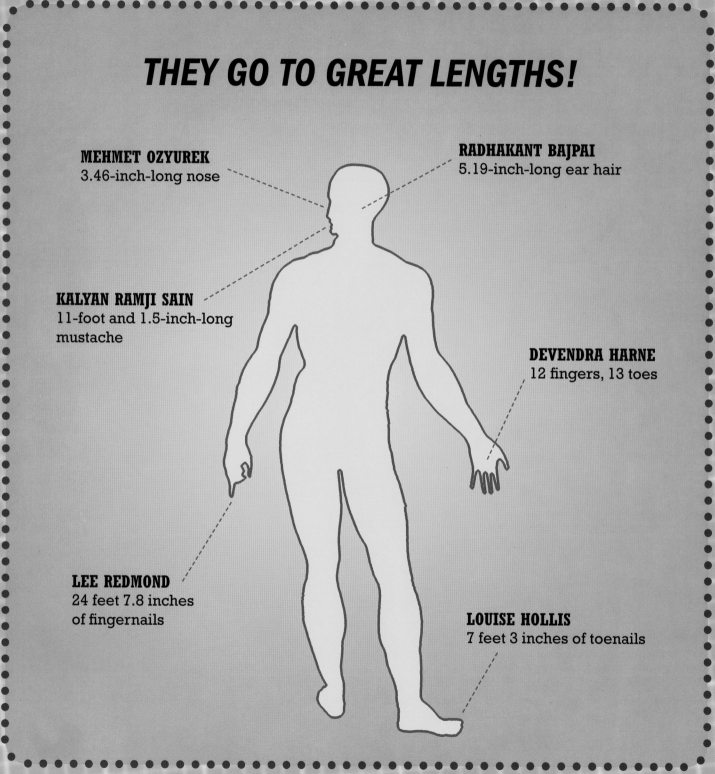

MEHMET OZYUREK
3.46-inch-long nose

RADHAKANT BAJPAI
5.19-inch-long ear hair

KALYAN RAMJI SAIN
11-foot and 1.5-inch-long mustache

DEVENDRA HARNE
12 fingers, 13 toes

LEE REDMOND
24 feet 7.8 inches of fingernails

LOUISE HOLLIS
7 feet 3 inches of toenails

LONGEST EAR HAIR

Growing the **LONGEST EAR HAIR** doesn't affect your hearing for better or worse, but it does earn a spot in the record books. Radhakant Bajpai is a 50-year-old grocer and dedicated family man living in Naya Ganj, Uttar Pradesh, India. A previous record-holder, fellow Indian B. D. Tyagi of Bhopal, inspired Radhakant to reconsider his own ear's naturally hairy extensions. As of May 2003, the strands sprouting from the middle of the pinna, or center of Radhakant's outer ears, stretched to an impressive 5.19 inches at their longest point! Dr. R. P. Gupta confirmed the measurements uprooted the previous record, and Radhakant became an official entrant into the archives. "Making it into *Guinness World Records* is indeed a special occasion for me and my family," he said.

DID YOU KNOW?

Although we hang earrings and rest eyeglasses upon the pinna (or auricle), its true purpose is to funnel sound into the ear canal.

TRIVIA TIDBITS

Our hair and earwax trap dirt and germs to protect the inner ear from infection.

73

HEAVIEST WEIGHT LIFTED WITH A HUMAN BEARD

Give Lithuanian Antanas Kontrimas's beard a tug and you'll be swept off your feet! This record-holder for whiskery feats of strength has strapped several items to the ends of his chin hairs and swung them clear off the ground, including a keg of his homemade beer, a sack of grain, a local TV host, and then the **HEAVIEST WEIGHT LIFTED WITH A HUMAN BEARD**. Antanas lifted a 139-pound girl 3.93 inches off the ground on the set of *Lo Show Dei Record* in Milan, Italy on January 5, 2006.

TRIVIA TIDBITS

The beard of Antanas Kontrimas has also towed a Land Rover, a sports plane, and a jeep with 5 passengers. He's training to lift a man and to haul in a fishing trawler.

DID YOU KNOW?

Antanas Kontrimas has not shaved for more than 25 years and his 20-inch beard is the longest in his hometown of Telshiai, Lithuania.

74

LONGEST MUSTACHE

Mustache care is more involved than beard growing, because the owner must clip and sometimes wax the mustache ends, also known as the tips. . . while a beard owner can just sit back and let nature take its course. Measuring a full beard is fairly straightforward for officials, and everybody else — done lengthwise, the ruler starts at the chin and finishes at the tip of the beard's longest whisker. Certifying the length of a mustache is a bit more divided, literally, by the nose. Measurements are still in length, but the ruler is used width-wise to determine the mustache's combined size in amount of hair grown on the right and left sides of the face.

Ram Singh Chauhan of India believes that someday he will be in the record books with his mustache. Yet he falls short of the record at the current length of only 6 feet 5 inches. The **LONGEST MUSTACHE** belongs to Kalyan Ramji Sain of India, who started his facial hair care in 1976. By measuring time in July 1993, his mustache had reached a record-setting span of 11 feet 1.5 inches. Although he is attentive to his hair's needs, the right side measured 5 feet 7 inches, while the left side was only 5 feet 6 inches.

TRIVIA TIDBITS

The previous mustachioed record-holder in India was Karna Ram Bheel, serving a life sentence in a New Delhi jail. In 1979, he tended all 7 feet 10 inches of his mustache with mustard, oil, butter, and cream.

DID YOU KNOW?

Genetics, diet, stress, and proper care affect all types of hair follicles responsible for healthy hair growth.

LONGEST COMBINED FINGERNAIL LENGTH

The nails covering our fingers and toes often give doctors a peek into our stomachs. How is that possible? Nails are a form of modified hair, with the plates of a nail made up of a protein called keratin. The nail bed is the connective tissue beneath the plate. Any serious illness will cause a groove in the nails known as Beau's lines. These grooves make the patient's medical history visible to the eye of a practiced doctor, nutritionist, and manicurist.

American Lee Redmond knows the secret of good nail care: You are what you eat. Lee eats plenty of protein and soaks her incredible fingernails in warm olive oil. She never chews on them — that would be a considerable meal because Lee has been letting her fingernails grow since 1979. She wanted to see how long she could grow her nails before they twisted . . . except they didn't, so she kept growing them, and growing, and growing. . . ! Her **LONGEST COMBINED FINGERNAIL LENGTH** is 24 feet 7.8 inches — prompting people to ask Lee, "Who does your nails?"

DID YOU KNOW?
Fingernails grow on average 0.02 inches per week — four times faster than their foot counterparts!

LONGEST TOENAILS

Another American woman decided she wanted pretty feet to show off in her fashionable summertime sandals, so she started growing out her toenails. In 1991, the **LONGEST TOENAILS** were a combined length of 87 inches — so each nail is approximately 6 inches long. . . and a different shade of toenail polish. Louise Hollis just couldn't bear to file those lovely nails down once the summer had ended. Her 12 children and 21 grandchildren lend a hand to help Louise paint and file her unique "collection." Louise enjoys the attention her colorful nails cause when she's out and about in her hometown of Compton, California.

DID YOU KNOW?

Nails and hair do not grow after death. The skin dehydrates, giving the appearance of longer nails and hair.

TRIVIA TIDBITS

Louise Hollis sassily chose her nails over a frustrated spouse when he gave her the ultimatum, "It's me or the nails!" Her reply, "I've had you for 21 years, but the nails are new."

GREATEST EAR SLINGSHOT

Monte Pierce of Bowling Green, Kentucky, holds an "ear-ie" talent. The human ear's auricle (or pinna) has no bone; its lower fatty part is the earlobe. Monte has been tugging on his earlobes all his life. The **LONGEST STRETCHED EARLOBES** can touch tips beneath Monte's chin, yet doctors determined Monte's hearing was unaffected by his stretching. He can stretch his right earlobe to 4.5 inches and his left to a full 5 inches!

Then Monte discovered his adjusted lobes had an extreme talent for lobbing. Monte builds up the skin's elastic energy by tugging on his earlobes. Then he places a coin on his ear and — just like a slingshot — lets go of the stretched lobe. The skin's built-up kinetic energy lobs the coin across the room. On October 29, 1999, Monte stretched his earlobe to nearly 5 inches and set a dime flying off it for a total distance of 10 feet 10.5 inches. This record for **GREATEST EAR SLINGSHOT** was set in the Los Angeles, California, studio of the *Guinness World Records: Primetime* TV show.

DID YOU KNOW?

The skin's elasticity allows the earlobes to snap back into place after being stretched — if done for brief amounts of time.

TRIVIA TIDBITS

The Suya tribespeople in Africa wear discs of wood in their ears to elongate them.

Quiz Me!

Test your *Extreme!* know-how with these cool quiz questions!

Q. #46
If polydactylism occurs in as many as 2 in every 1,000 births, who are some famous polydactyls?

Q. #47
Edmond Rostand's *Cyrano de Bergerac* is a famous play about a sensitive guy with a huge nose. Has it ever been made into a movie?

Q. #48
Radhakant Bajpai grew the **Longest Ear Hair**, but does everyone have ear hair?

Q. #49
Antanas Kontrimas has a record-breaking beard. Which of the following fictional characters also have famous beards?
a) Gandalf from J.R.R. Tolkien's *The Lord of the Rings*
b) Papa Smurf (from the *Smurfs*)
c) Dumbledore from *Harry Potter*
d) All of the above

Q. #50
We know that the hair that grows on the top of your lip is known as a "mustache," but what is a "mustachio"?
a) A type of Turkish car
b) A flavor of ice cream
c) A term for a large mustache
d) None of the above

Q. #51
What is the name for those white spots that you sometimes see under your fingernails?

Q. #52
Louise Hollis certainly knows how to pamper her toenails, but is painting your toenails or getting a pedicure a modern phenomenon?

Q. #53
Are there cultures where stretched earlobes, like Monte Pierce's, are desired?

EXTREME

TEETH

Teeth are primarily for chewing and, in extreme cases, **ATTACK AND DEFENSE.** In this category of toothy competitors, the bravest dentist would have nightmares after seeing how these record-breakers strain the limits of good dental care.

STRONGEST BITE

Do you know where the strongest muscle in your body is located? In your mouth! The masseter muscle controls the jaw's movements in talking, chewing, and biting. The "bite force" is the amount of pressure applied by the masseter upon an object. Scientists measure these levels using a bite-meter (or gnathodynamometer).

The Lerner Marine Laboratory in the Bahamas recorded the **STRONGEST BITE** using a bite-meter designed just for sharks. Marine biologists tested tiger, lemon, and dusky sharks by stuffing the meter inside a mackerel. At 6 feet 6.75 inches long, the dusky shark (*Carcharhinus obscurus*) registered a force of 132 pounds of pressure between its jaws. At the tip of its teeth, that equals 22 *tons* of pressure. That's the same as being crushed by 10 cars!

Curious about the bite force of the **LARGEST PREDATORY FISH**? So are biologists because, in theory, a bigger animal should exert a higher bite force. . . but no one has yet recorded any official measurements between the jaws of the biggest fish, the great white shark. Meanwhile, paleontologists are learning more about evolution through the reconstruction and bite-force tests of fossilized dinosaur jaws.

DID YOU KNOW?

The great white shark can grow to more than 15 feet long. It has several rows of teeth, with approximately 3,000 sharp replacements for the teeth lost every week.

TRIVIA TIDBITS

Marine biologist James Snodgrass designed the bite-meter for sharks: the Snodgrass gnathodynamometer. (Try saying that fast 10 times!)

TOOTHSOME TRIVIA

While the Largest and Strongest teeth have their place, what about the average? The average adult human has thirty-two teeth (if they brush!) But among the animal kingdom, we are just one of many species.

• Turtles and tortoises are toothless. Instead of teeth, they use their horn-covered jaws to tear food into small enough pieces to swallow.

• Giraffes, like humans, have 32 teeth. Giraffes' teeth have deep grooves for stripping foliage from twigs.

• Crocodiles and alligators have 60 to 80 teeth respectively, but can grow up to 2,000-3,000 teeth during their lifetime. When a crocodile or alligator wears down their teeth, they can shed and regrow them. Over a lifetime, a crocodile can produce 40 sets of teeth!

• Giant armadillos' 100 teeth are largely wasted. These insect and plant eaters consume food whole, using their long mucus-covered tongues to digest food.

• Dolphins can average having 200 small, sharply pointed teeth, ideal for grasping slippery fish and squid.

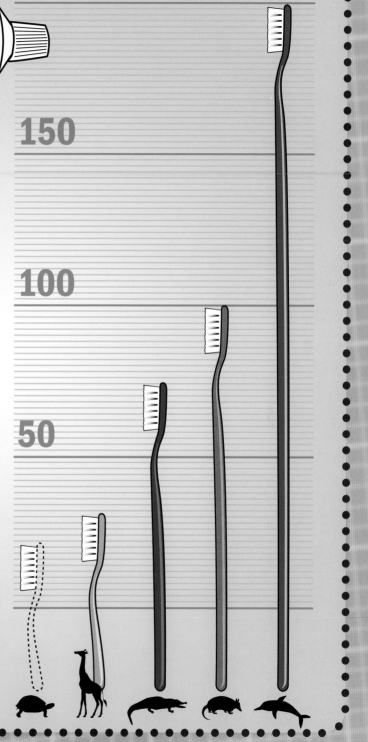

HEAVIEST VEHICLE PULLED WITH TEETH

Humans grow two sets of teeth in a lifetime. The first set of 20 "milk" teeth arrive during the teething stage of 6 months old. The second set — growing beneath the first — pushes out the old ones, tooth by tooth, between the ages of 6 to 12 years old. Since the adult set of 32 teeth is your *final* natural set, your dentist isn't kidding about the importance of taking good care of your teeth.

Dentists might not approve of these record-holders' toothy hobby of weight lifting. On March 31, 1990, Walter Arfeuille earned his record for, **GREATEST WEIGHT LIFTED BY TEETH** in Paris, France. Walter held a total weight of 620 pounds 10 ounces off the ground by a distance of 6.75 inches. On October 18, 2003, Velu Rathakrishnan broke Walter's previous record of **HEAVIEST VEHICLE PULLED WITH TEETH** at Kuala Lumpur Railway Station, Maylasia. Velu pulled two KTM commuter trains, weighing an astonishing total of 287.48 tons, for a distance of 13 feet 9 inches!

HEAVIEST SHIP PULLED BY TEETH

Archeologists have dug up the truth about dentists: Ancient civilizations knew about and practiced dental surgery. This included the forceful removal of diseased teeth with primitive tools. Somehow this knowledge, dating back to the Indus Valley civilization of 3300 BCE, was lost during the confusion of the Middle Ages. This was a time when people would visit a "barber surgeon" to have hair cut, beards shaved, *and* teeth pulled. Another alternative was a "tooth drawer," a performance artist who yanked a patient's teeth for others' entertainment. Today, people visit licensed dentists for the proper care and removal of problematic teeth.

Omar Hanapiev from Russia hopes to never lose a tooth by any of these methods since he depends on each and every one — plus several muscles — during his record attempts. Just like Velu and trains, Omar specializes in being a tooth-tower of vehicles. On November 9, 2001, he set the record for **HEAVIEST SHIP PULLED BY TEETH**. Omar towed the tanker *Gunib* a distance of 49 feet 2.4 inches in the port of Makhachkala, Russia. A rope tied his teeth to a ship weighing 576 tons (or 1,269,861 pounds). People cheered that day because he didn't lose a single tooth.

LARGEST MAMMAL JAW

A multiple record-holder for its astonishing size, the sperm whale (*Physeter macrocephalus*) on average grows to between 40 to 65 feet long. A male specimen, tipping the scales at nearly 84 feet, yielded a lower jaw of 16 feet 5 inches in length! The **LARGEST MAMMAL JAW** was exhibited in London's Natural History Museum. As you would guess, sperm whales are also the **LARGEST-TOOTHED WHALES**. Although the teeth in the upper jaw never erupt through the gums, the lower jaw contains about 50 to 60 conical-shaped teeth. Each tooth is approximately 7 inches long and weighs 2 pounds! When the whale shuts its mouth, its massive lower teeth fit snugly into sockets located in the upper jaw.

The sperm whale swims in the open oceans, except for the chilly polar seas, and is capable of diving to the greatest depths on a hunt for giant squid, another oversize record-holder. In 1991, a sperm whale dove to a depth of 6,500 feet in the Caribbean Sea. The **DEEPEST RECORD DIVE BY A MAMMAL** lasted for 1 hour 13 minutes. The **LARGEST ANIMAL BRAIN**, at 19 pounds 13 ounces, also fits inside this whale's truly big head.

DID YOU KNOW?

Think the sperm whale is the biggest fish in the sea? Wrong times two! Whales are mammals that breathe air and are not classified as fish. The **LARGEST MAMMAL** is the blue whale, bigger than any dinosaur skeleton. One male blue whale measured 90 feet 6 inches in length and weighed 420,000 pounds.

LAND MAMMAL WITH THE MOST TEETH

Mammals are a classification of warm-blooded animals having backbones, hair-covered skin, and the ability to bear their children alive instead of laying eggs. Thankfully, the **LAND MAMMAL WITH THE MOST TEETH** isn't interested in taking a bite out of us. The giant armadillo (*Priodontes maximus*) uses its approximately 100 teeth lining the inside of its long snout for pest population maintenance. It is nature's biggest exterminator of termites and ants, yet today it is also one of the most endangered animals. It has been overhunted for its meat and killed by farmers mistaking it as a crop eater. Found in South America, the giant armadillo burrows through soil in search of bugs and a nesting place.

These amazing creatures are recognized by a distinctive armored shell, but the giant armadillo is too large at 35 inches to curl its massive underbelly beneath its armor. Instead, it owns the **LARGEST CLAWS** of the animal kingdom. Its front, central claws measure 8 inches long. The armadillo uses both teeth and claws to rip apart the termite mounds towering throughout the region or to dig a fast getaway tunnel.

> ## DID YOU KNOW?
> Copra is the edible white meat inside of the coconut and is used to make coconut oil.

TRIVIA TIDBITS
Certain species of armadillo spend 80 percent of their lives either dozing or asleep.

FASTEST TIME TO HUSK A COCONUT USING ONLY TEETH

Rajesh Prabhu, a 26-year-old man of Bahrain, India, was having a bad day until he saw a monkey trying to open a coconut. Rajesh wondered if any human had tried to husk a coconut in the same efficient manner: using hands, feet, and teeth. Then Rajesh learned about Sidaraju S. Raju, the record-holder for **FASTEST TIME TO HUSK A COCONUT USING ONLY TEETH**.

Sidaraju comes from a family of farmers in Magadi, India. His love of trying new things led to applying his teeth in a unique manner. On March 30, 2003, Sidaraju sunk his teeth into the brown fiber containing the fruit of the coconut palm tree. The coconut measured 30.7 inches and weighed 10 pounds 6.4 ounces. Within 28.06 seconds, the husk was gone and Sidaraju had entered the record books.

Quiz Me!

**Test your *Extreme!* know-how
with these cool quiz questions!**

Q. #54
True or False? Ounce for ounce, the masseter muscle is the strongest muscle in your body.

Q. #55
Record holders for tooth-tugging vehicles need strong teeth. Not brushing or flossing can lead to which of the following dental problems?
a) Halitosis
b) Gingivitis
c) Periodontitis
d) All of the above

Q. #56
True or False? People used to believe that pulling out bad teeth would cure other illnesses.

Q. #57
The sperm whale has the largest jaw, teeth, and brain, and is capable of diving deeper than other animals in search of food. Do all of these record-breaking features guarantee a long life?

Q. #58
The giant armadillo is the **Land Mammal with the Most Teeth**. Are its teeth very sharp?

Q. #59
When Rajesh Prabhu saw a monkey husk a coconut, it inspired him to try the same with his teeth. So can monkeys be trained to harvest coconuts?

EXTREME

FOOD

Multiple competitive events focusing on food — the art of its preparation, the speed in its cooking, and the amount one human can consume — have sprouted in popularity around the globe. Our focus is on several record-breaking **CULINARY MASTERPIECES** that tip the weight scales before anyone takes a single bite.

LONGEST HOT DOG

Several European cities — from Frankfurt, Germany, to Vienna, Austria — lay claim to creating the cooked sausage sandwich. Historical accounts of who, where, and when these red-hot, little-dog wieners in a bun were first introduced to the American people is still in debate. Everyone does agree on the hot dog's top spot in popular food items. July is America's National Hot Dog month because a jaw-dropping 150 million hot dogs are eaten during thousands of Independence Day celebrations.

The **LONGEST HOT DOG** measured 57.5 feet and was made by Conshohocken Bakery and Berks Meat Packing for the 20th Annual Corvettes for Kids fundraiser in Bally, Pennsylvania on August 14, 2005. Conshohoken Bakery not only donated a super-sized bun but also purchased the hot dog for $250. The hot dog was cut into pieces, then grilled and sold to benefit the fundraiser.

TRIVIA TIDBITS

Americans eat an estimated 7 *billion* hot dogs between Memorial Day and Labor Day!

DID YOU KNOW?

Applying mustard, relish, onions, and more condiments to a hot dog is called "dragging it through the garden."

LARGEST ICE-CREAM SUNDAE

Having trouble deciding which flavor to choose for your sundae at the local ice cream parlor? Imagine scooping enough ice cream to create a sundae weighing 25 tons! That's what it would take to break the current record held by the Edmonton, Canada-based Palm Dairies for sculpting the **LARGEST ICE-CREAM SUNDAE**. On July 24, 1988, this gigantic confection officially weighed 54,914 pounds!

Controversy swirls around several claims of inventing the first ice-cream sundae. The definition of a sundae is a serving of ice cream with a topping (syrup, fruit, nuts, or whipped cream). The choice and amount of its sweet ingredients depend on a person's likes and dislikes. Purists claim it all comes down to a scoop of vanilla beneath chocolate syrup. The whipped cream and cherry on top are extraneous. Thomas Jefferson reportedly favored maple syrup on his vanilla ice cream, yet no one called his after-dinner snack a "sundae."

Chilled treats made from the milk of horses, buffalo, yaks, camels, cows, and goats have been traced to China's T'ang Dynasty (618–907 AD). Americans discovered the popular frozen dessert sometime in the 1770s. Today, the USA makes more than 1.5 billion gallons of ice cream a year.

LARGEST COLLECTION OF POTATO CHIP BAGS

People love to collect things because the item — a postcard, matchbook, or ticket stub — reminds them of their pleasant experience at that vacation spot, restaurant, or event. These souvenirs range from childhood toys to expensive antiques, from zany buttons to colorful traffic cones. Collections are as unique as collectors, who consider the search for, and finding of, new items a serious personal quest.

Bernd Sikora of Germany started his collection in 1993, and the record really is "in the bag." Today, he owns 1,482 potato chip bags from 43 countries. This is the **LARGEST COLLECTION OF POTATO CHIP BAGS** known in existence. The saying is true — Bernd could not stop after "just one."

> **DID YOU KNOW?**
> Potato chips were stored in tins or barrels before the invention of the airtight, sealed bag.

LARGEST GINGERBREAD MAN

Gingerbread can be rolled and patted and shaped into edible figures of people, animals, and houses. These ginger-flavored cookies, bread, and cakes have a baking history dating back to the eleventh century in Western Europe. Such treats were made and sold at local fairs, with many customs and fanciful tales passed down about the eating of gingerbread.

The **LARGEST GINGERBREAD MAN** did not come from Germany, a country rich in traditions, fairy tales, and recipes for gingerbread. Instead, Canada unveiled this gigantic cookie on November 19, 2003. Chefs working at the Hyatt Regency Hotel in Vancouver baked and presented a gingerbread man measuring 13 feet 11 inches tall, 5 feet 8 inches wide, and 2 inches deep. He weighed 372 pounds 13 ounces!

A baker and his team from Rochester, Minnesota, are hoping to catch this record with their attempt at the 2006 Baker's Convention. John Fish of the Gingerbread House Bakery hopes the 14-foot 11-inch gingerbread man stays intact, since no parts are allowed to break off and run away before the measurements are complete.

RECIPE FOR A RECORD-BREAKER

- 222 pounds 14 ounces of flour
- 44 pounds of shortening
- 44 pounds of white sugar
- 44 pounds of molasses (refined sugar syrup)
- 8 pounds 8 ounces of ground ginger
- 6 pounds 4 ounces of baking soda
- 6 pounds 4 ounces of sea salt
- 6 pounds 4 ounces of ground nutmeg

LARGEST POPCORN SCULPTURE

Godzilla and King Kong are battling each other again! This time, the icons of movie monster films are fighting for the title of **LARGEST POPCORN SCULPTURE**. The great ape held the title on July 24, 2003. Leicester Square's Odeon Cinema in London commissioned a kernel King Kong in celebration of the original 1933 film's 70th anniversary. The final sculpture stood 13 feet tall and 8 feet 9 inches wide.

Then the giant reptile had its day on October 3, 2003. Carlton Cinema in Stirling, UK, was celebrating 65 years of entertaining moviegoers with films and the favorite concession treat of popped corn kernels. Edinburgh artist Emma Herman-Smith sculpted Godzilla from millions of popcorn pieces in her city studio. . . and then took him apart for reassembly on the theater's roof. Workers waved off insects buzzing around the sweet, sticky sculpture that rose 16 feet 0.5 inches into the sky.

The fight isn't over yet. We've heard about culinary and engineering students at Michigan's Grand Rapids Community College cooking up a recipe for a 25-foot-tall King Kong, this time atop the Empire State Building. Good luck popping the record!

DID YOU KNOW?
Pieces of 4,000-year-old popcorn were found in the "Bat Cave" of New Mexico.

RECIPE FOR A RECORD-BREAKER
(a 25-foot King Kong requires these ingredients)
- 600 pounds of popcorn
- 500 pounds of adhesive
- 200 hours of sculpting

TRIVIA TIDBITS
Popcorn artisans recommend melted marshmallows or resin as an adhesive for keeping the kernels stuck together. Marion, Ohio, hosts an annual popcorn festival every September that attracts an estimated 250,000 kernel enthusiasts!

LARGEST ANNUAL FOOD FIGHT

Food fights are messy fun when you're in the middle of one, but everyone dreads the clean-up. Consider living in the town of Buñol, Spain. Since 1944, a weeklong celebration there at the end of August has paid tribute to the town's patron saint, Saint Louis, with parties, fireworks, and parades. The good time culminates in *La Tomatina*, the **LARGEST ANNUAL FOOD FIGHT**. The end of tomato-growing season yields tons of surplus tomatoes perfect for squishing and throwing among excited citizens and tourists. Tomato juice stains the crowds and runs 12 inches deep through the crowded streets. In 2002, the fruity festival hit a milestone — *splat!* — when 38,000 people threw a total sum of 275,000 pounds of tomatoes.

TRIVIA TIDBITS
How did this wild food fight start? The clouded origins include mischievous boys and spilled fruit carts. Tomatoes ended up being thrown and the annual tradition stuck.

Quiz Me!

Test your *Extreme!* know-how with these cool quiz questions!

Q. #60
Americans are huge hot dog fans, and no place is better for a hot dog than a baseball game. Which US baseball stadium sold the most hot dogs in 2005?
a) Dodger Stadium
b) Yankee Stadium
c) Wrigley Field
d) Coors Field

Q. #61
Although the origins of the ice cream sundae are obscure and disputed, what US city claims to be the "Home of the Ice Cream Sundae"?

Q. #62
Bernd Sikora certainly likes his potato chips. What US state should he thank for their potatoes?

Q. #63
True or False? Ginger can calm an upset stomach.

Q. #64
Giant statues of Godzilla and King Kong have been sculpted out of popcorn. Has there ever been a movie made where these two fictional monsters actually fight each other?

Q. #65
Food fights are often thought of as taking place in school cafeterias, but in what country's legislature did a food fight erupt in 2004?
a) Zimbabwe
b) The United States
c) Taiwan
d) Greenland

EXTREME

LUXURIES

No matter how much people complain about the cost of living, there will always be those **BIG SPENDERS** willing to pay extravagant amounts for the shiniest, priciest, and oddest objects just because they must own them! The price tags of these pursuits break records and bank accounts.

DINING OUT AT THE HIGHEST ALTITUDE

True friendship is priceless and doesn't have limits. . . but sometimes safety harnesses are in order. A group of experienced mountain climbers took formal dining to new heights on May 3, 2004. Seven out of a ten-member expedition dressed for **DINING OUT AT THE HIGHEST ALTITUDE** by wearing tuxedos as they trudged out from base camp. Their destination: a friend's 30th birthday dinner with a killer view from the top of Lhakpa Ri, Tibet.

The mountaineers, including a professional butler, scaled the summit carrying tables, chairs, silver cutlery, flowers, candelabras, and a five-course meal. Hurricane winds at the peak relocated their dining site a few feet lower on the mountain — at an astonishing 22,326 feet! Henry Shelford was the guest of honor. Joshua Heming served caviar, smoked duck, chocolate bombe, cheese, wine, and birthday cake to the extreme diners: Thomas Shelford, Nakul Misra Pathak, Robert Aitken, Robert Sully (all UK), and Caio Buzzolini (Australia). Everyone ate and made merry, until they realized the climb back down was still ahead.

MOST EXPENSIVE CAR REGISTRATION

Folklores in different cultures claim good luck will be yours upon finding certain objects, such as a heads-side-up penny or a four-leaf clover — or performing specific activities, such as tossing spilled salt over a shoulder or knocking on wood. Many cultures believe that certain numbers are lucky (7) or unlucky (13).

Buying an object to guarantee your good fortune might cost you a fortune! On March 19, 1994, a government auction in Hong Kong, China, sold the **MOST EXPENSIVE CAR REGISTRATION** to an eager buyer for a staggering amount of money. Albert Yeung Sau-shing paid $13 million for one car license plate. The plate simply stated "9" and nothing else. The word "nine" is identical to "dog" in Cantonese pronunciation, and according to cultural logic, this specific license plate was extremely lucky to own in 1994, the Year of the Dog.

DID YOU KNOW?

The printing of license plates for any type of vehicle, and the associated rules of registration, are different in every part of the world.

TRIVIA TIDBITS

The Chinese zodiac has 12 animal signs and each animal is repeated every 12 years. The Year of the Dog repeated in 2006, with its next return scheduled for 2018.

MOST VALUABLE COMIC

Comic books developed from cartoons printed in newspapers during the late nineteenth century. A series of "comic strips" were collected and printed in a magazine form that was called a "comic book." This new art form became incredibly popular during World War II because the format weighed less than hardback books, had lots of colorful pictures, was easy to read, and cost only a few pennies.

Today's best-known comic book publishers are DC Comics and Marvel Comics. Their band of recognizable superheroes — Batman, Superman, X-Men, and the Fantastic Four — have soared in popularity, with these adventures now appearing in comic books, novels, animated TV shows, and movies.

THE MOST VALUABLE COMIC is the 1939 first edition of Marvel Comics. Jay Parrino's The Mint, a company dealing in rare coins, comics, and photographs based in Kansas City, Missouri, paid $350,000 for "Pay Copy" *Marvel Comics No. 1* in November 2001. This edition was called the "pay copy" because its cover and seven pages listed the artist and pay scale. For example, artist Frank R. Paul received only $25 for his now-legendary cover.

MOST VALUABLE BASEBALL CARD

In 1903, a historic series of baseball games were played between the Pittsburgh Pirates and the Boston Americans. At the time, this unnamed competition consisted of nine games, with the championship team determined by the most games won. The Boston team won the fifth game and the championship with Game 8. This challenge would become the famous World Series. The Pirate shortstop during the inaugural game was Honus Wagner, who would become a member of the Baseball Hall of Fame and the sought-after face on the **MOST VALUABLE BASEBALL CARD**.

In 1909, the Pirates were playing against the Detroit Tigers for the World Series title. Candy and tobacco companies promoted this beloved sport inside their packages by giving away cardboard cards printed with the players' names and faces. Card number 486 in a 514-card set known as the T206 series featured Honus Wagner — and he was not happy about it. Honus reportedly was upset that his face was being used to promote the sale of tobacco to kids. His card became a rare find among collectors. So rare, in fact, that even in the 1930s, his 50-cent card sold for 50 dollars. On July 15, 2000, one of these rare cards surfaced during an online eBay auction. American Brian Seigal paid the price of $1,265,000 for this elusive piece of baseball history.

WAGNER, PITTSBURG

TRIVIA TIDBITS
An uncut printer's sheet featuring Honus Wagner's card was supposedly found folded up in an old baseball uniform also belonging to Wagner.

MOST VALUABLE DINOSAUR BONES

Owning a piece of history is a costly, and valuable, investment — especially if the purchase is made for the benefit of future generations. On August 12, 1990, explorers from South Dakota's Black Hills Institute for Geological Research were exploring the foothills when they stumbled across a gigantic discovery: the **LARGEST AND MOST COMPLETE TYRANNOSAURUS REX SKELETON**. The skeleton was 90 percent complete and measured 13 feet tall and 41 feet long.

Nicknamed "Sue," the dinosaur's bones sparked a debate of ownership among the land's owners, the town, the researchers, and the American government. Finally, after numerous legal battles, a judge determined Sue's skeleton and any monies from its sale belonged to the private rancher who owned the land. Sue was sold at the famous auction house of Sotheby's in New York on October 4, 1997. A group of sponsors donated funds to help The Field Museum of Chicago, Illinois, afford the $8,362,500 price tag. But the sticker shock was worth it, because the **MOST VALUABLE DINOSAUR BONES** have fascinated millions, young and old, since going on display at museums across America.

MOST EXPENSIVE CHOCOLATE BAR

A bar of chocolate can be purchased at many convenient places, such as vending machines, for a handful of coins. Captain Robert Falcon Scott desperately needed any type of food, especially that quick rush of sugar and caffeine provided by chocolate, during his second fateful trip to the South Pole. This doomed expedition wiped out all of Scott's supplies, and he and his entire crew perished in 1912.

However, on his first exploration of Antarctica from 1901 to 1904, Scott and his men had plenty of chocolate. They towed 3,500 pounds of cocoa and chocolate on their frigid trek. Many bars survived, including a piece only 4 inches long. This prized bite of history fetched $687 at a special Polar Expeditions auction held by Christie's of London. An anonymous buyer bought the **MOST EXPENSIVE CHOCOLATE BAR** on September 25, 2001.

THIS BAR OF CHOCOLATE WAS TAKEN FROM THE BOAT "DISCOVERY" ON ITS RETURN FROM CAPT. SCOTTS EXPEDITION TO ATTEMPT TO REACH THE SOUTH POLE IN 1905

DID YOU KNOW?
Sir Ernest Shackleton, also a famous Antarctic explorer, journeyed with Scott during part of the 1901-1904 expedition.

MOST EXPENSIVE ELEPHANT PAINTING

Do you remember the orchestral members of gigantic proportions? Those talented musicians performed at the Thai Elephant Conservation Center in Lampang, Thailand. The center also runs an elephant hospital and training school. Thai elephants in captivity were mainly used in moving huge trees for the logging industry. But in 1989, when the government changed its laws regarding this business, unemployed *mahouts* and their elephants went to the school for help in learning a new career. Some elephants picked up a musical instrument. Other elephants picked up a paintbrush.

A group of these talented painters created a masterpiece titled *Cold Wind, Swirling Mist, Charming Lanna I.* The viewing and sale of this unusual painting was held on February 19, 2005, at the Maesa Elephant Camp in Chiang Mai, Thailand. The **MOST EXPENSIVE ELEPHANT PAINTING** sold for $39,000 to Phanit Warin, formerly of Chiang Mai, now living in northern California. All monies are donated to the care and conservation of Thailand's elephants.

TRIVIA TIDBITS

In 1997, Russian-born artists Vitaly Komar and Alex Melamid journeyed to Thailand and became art teachers for the elephants.

DID YOU KNOW?

An elephant trainer is a *mahout*.

MOST EXPENSIVE COMMERCIALLY AVAILABLE DOMESTIC ROBOT

The way of the future is a world filled with mechanical helpers. Robots range in size and function between miniscule search engines in our computers to average-size humanoids designed not only to look "more human" in appearance but to mimic our actions. These extreme machines can talk, walk, run, lift, dance, and survive in the harshest environmental climates — from volcanic pits to the vacuum of outer space. The latest models resemble our household pets, free of allergy-causing hair and with a bark-mute mode. Will these metallic wonders provide the same comfort level as our families and furry friends?

Thames, a Japanese manufacturer, broke through into the household market with their TMSUK IV robot. This "woman in a dress"-shaped robot specializes in household care and personal assistance. It first rolled across the public stage on January 23, 2000, during a robotics show held in Tokyo, Japan. The 220-pound robot stands 4 feet tall, with an original price tag of $43,037. Today, inflation has raised the price tag to $49,508! The **MOST EXPENSIVE COMMERCIALLY AVAILABLE DOMESTIC ROBOT** runs errands, never complains, is trained in giving massages to humans, and can be operated by remote control.

MOST EXPENSIVE TRIP TO SPACE BY A TOURIST

A little more than a century ago, the idea of people paying to fly on gigantic planes across the country was believed to be an impossible dream. Today, the skies are filled with passenger-crowded jets operated by many different airlines. Cars, boats, and trains are everyday modes of transportation. But what about trips around the moon?

American businessman Dennis Tito wanted a phenomenal vacation and paid the steep price of $20 million to Russia for a visit to the International Space Station (ISS). A former NASA engineer, Dennis blasted off on April 28, 2001. He spent six days floating around the station, snapping photos of Earth, peering out the portholes, and listening to opera. He splashed down on May 6, 2001, with plenty of souvenirs of the **MOST EXPENSIVE TRIP TO SPACE BY A TOURIST**.

The following year, South African Internet millionaire Mark Shuttleworth also paid Russia the same price for the same amount of time spent visiting the ISS. He took off on April 25, 2002, and landed on May 5, 2002. Is this the first step toward a family vacation on Mars?

DID YOU KNOW?
Wall-mounted sleeping bags on the ISS prevent sleepers from walking or floating away in the gravity-free environment.

Quiz Me!

Test your *Extreme!* know-how with these cool quiz questions!

Q. #66
Henry Shelford and his friends ate opposite the famous Mount Everest. Why is Mount Everest such a formidable challenge to climbers?

Q. #67
The number 13 is often considered unlucky, but do people actually fear it?

Q. #68
A series of comic strips printed as a collection is called a comic book. But what's another name for a longer, more complex, comic book?

Q. #69
What are the only two companies that currently produce major league baseball cards?

Q. #70
"Sue" is the current record-holder for **Most Valuable Dinosaur Bones**. What does the name *Tyrannosaurus Rex* literally mean?
a) Thunder Lizard
b) King Tyrant Lizard
c) Deceptive Lizard
d) None of the above

Q. #71
Everybody loves chocolate, right? However, what country consumes more chocolate per capita than any other nation?
a) Switzerland
b) The United States of America
c) Belgium
d) Mexico

Q. #72
The elephants of the Thai Elephant Conservation Center are not only talented musicians, but also talented (not to mention expensive!) painters. Where can you see a selection of elephant art?

Q. #73
TMSUK IV is the **Most Expensive Commercially Available Domestic Robot**. You may have heard of the AIBO®, a robot that is designed to look and act like a dog. Which of the following can the AIBO® do?
a) Recognize more than 100 words
b) House sit by using video and photo recording
c) Lick your face when you wake up in the morning
d) Both "a" and "b"

Q. #74
True or False? Since Mark Shuttleworth's trip to space, the International Space Station has stopped having tourists come to space.

EXTREME

APPETITES

The table manners and diets of these record-holders would turn heads in any restaurant, especially when one of them **DEVOURS THE SILVERWARE** instead of the food on his plate!

MOST WORMS EATEN IN 30 SECONDS

How much could you eat in 30 seconds? Proper dining etiquette — and your frowning parent — forbids the gobbling of a meal. But every second counts in record-breaking. The type of food in the bowl will greatly affect your attempt's success or failure. Which kind of meal do you think would be easier to swallow: solid, round candies eaten with a chopstick or hundreds of wiggly, slimy earthworms with no silverware allowed?

If your name was C. Manoharan, better known by his friends as "Snake" Manu, then option No. 2 is your best bet. A twenty-something man from Tandaiarpet, India, "Snake" Manu got his nickname after years of fascination with reptiles. After a while, he taste-tested one and it became his favorite meal. "Snake" Manu had no problem with a bowl full of 200 live earthworms. He simply tipped the bowl up to his lips and — *gulp!* — swallowed its entire contents and the record for **MOST WORMS EATEN IN 30 SECONDS**. Each freshly picked earthworm measured at least 4 inches long and was fully consumed within the time limit. "Snake" Manu enjoyed his homegrown meal in Chennai City, India on November 15, 2003.

FASTEST ENTRAPMENT BY A PLANT

The land-based Venus flytrap and its underwater cousin, the bladderwort plant, invite plenty of bugs to dinner — as the main course. These carnivores catch lots of flies and microscopic aquatic creatures. The bladderwort plant catches its meals on the water's current, but the Venus flytrap creates a honey-type substance called nectar. The sticky and sweet liquid tempts a hungry bug right inside the plant's mouth.

The "mouth" of both plants is really a two-hinged leaf with teeth. The upper surface of the leaf is lined with sensitive hair cells that are triggered by a bug's movements. When an insect triggers two of these cells in a row, the leaf snaps shut and the "trap" is sprung. The plant secretes special enzymes to digest the insect providing the plant with the nitrogen it needs to grow. The Venus flytrap "swallows" its prey in one-tenth of a second while the bladderwort plant closes its hidden trapdoor in just $\frac{1}{15,000}$th of a second. These two will never share a meal, but they do share the record for **FASTEST ENTRAPMENT BY A PLANT**, split between land-and water-based diners.

TRIVIA TIDBITS

The bladderwort plant (*Utricularia vulgaris*) is rootless and floats upon the surface of ponds, marshes, and tropical waters.

DID YOU KNOW?

The Venus flytrap (*Dionaea muscipula*) grows on the coastal plains of North and South Carolina.

WHAT'S ON THE MENU?

Take your stomach on a tour around the world.
Here's a sample of other people's favorite dishes!

APPETIZERS

★ In Japan, ketchup is poured over rice.

★ An expensive Russian delicacy, caviar, comes from fish eggs.

★ Locust swarms feed a lot of people. Cambodians pop a peanut inside the bug and panfry it.

★ Salted licorice is a popular candy in Holland and Sweden.

MAIN COURSE

★ Seaweed is dried and eaten in the Philippines and Japan.

★ In Thailand, giant water bugs are served with chili and sticky rice. Dung beetles add spice to curry dishes.

★ Black pudding, a breakfast dish in the UK, is made by cooking pig's blood until it solidifies.

★ Sheep heads are skinned, broiled, and eaten in parts of the Mediterranean.

★ In Barbados, flying fish is a breaded, panfried dish *and* a symbol in the country's crest.

★ People cook and eat armadillo meat in areas of Central and South America.

STRANGEST DIET

Diet fads come and go every week. The sensible diet is a healthy one approved by your personal doctor that combines the right amount of daily exercise with balanced meals of proteins, vegetables, fruits, starches, calories, and vitamins. So you probably shouldn't partake in the **STRANGEST DIET** from Monsieur Mangetout.

Michel Lotito of Grenoble, France, is better known as Monsieur Mangetout, the man who can safely eat and completely digest metal and glass. Since 1959, Mangetout has been consuming a daily average of 2 pounds of metal. By October 1997, estimates placed the total amount of metal consumed by him at a whopping 9 tons! Although doctors have analyzed his digestion and learned his gastric juices have a metal-corrosive foam, they still are unable to explain how this man's body has digested the following metallic morsels: 18 bicycles, 15 shopping carts, 7 TV sets, 6 chandeliers, 2 beds, a pair of skis, a computer, and a Cessna light aircraft. He also managed to devour an empty coffin.

MOST HAMBURGERS STUFFED IN THE MOUTH

The hamburger is a popular meal around the world. But just holding a sandwich in your mouth *without* biting down, chewing, or swallowing? You might choke — remember, record-breaking can be dangerous!

The **MOST HAMBURGERS STUFFED IN THE MOUTH** requires more than three regulation-size sandwiches (including buns and condiments) to be held in the mouth at the same time and the participant is not allowed to swallow any part of the hamburgers. That dog named Augie would gladly give up his tennis balls to hold one hamburger in his mouth, but this is a human-only competition. American Johnny Reitz first performed his cheek-stretching feat on the set of the TV show *Guinness World Records: Primetime*, in Los Angeles, California, on June 17, 1998. He set the record at three hamburgers.

DID YOU KNOW?
The citizens of Hamburg, Germany, enjoyed a ground beef patty sandwich called a "Hamburg steak" in the late nineteenth century.

TRIVIA TIDBITS
At the 2004 Singaporean World Record Contest, competitors also tried — and failed — to break the fastest-drinking-ketchup-through-a-straw record set in 1999 by Dustin Phillips.

FASTEST TOMATO KETCHUP DRINKER

It seems that no one really *can* catch up to the "ketchup king"! American Dustin Phillips set the record for **FASTEST TOMATO KETCHUP DRINKER** back in 1999. Although many have tried, no one has yet out-slurped him.

Dustin liked ketchup, lots of it, on his food. One night at dinner, friends dared him to drink the rest of the ketchup bottle. That was back in college, and his first attempt resulted in quite a mess. But then he began practicing, whetting the taste buds daily with a full bottle, until his skills were unmatched.

On September 23, 1999, Dustin went to Los Angeles, California, intent on sharing his talent with the world. Dustin took the stage on the set of the TV show *Guinness World Records: Primetime*. The drinking straw was 0.25 inches in diameter. The bottle was one standard 14-ounce Heinz® Tomato Ketchup bottle. Dustin slurped 91 percent of the bottle's contents through his straw within 33 seconds.

LARGEST BARBECUE

Eating is a social activity dating back to prehistoric people huddling around a fire. Perhaps the origins of the barbecue can be traced back to those ancient days? Slow-cooking meat on an open flame is one of the most popular and easiest methods of preparing food. Worldwide, cities hold gigantic events in the hopes of being declared the new record-holder for **LARGEST BARBECUE**.

A gigantic group of Australians threw the biggest bash at Warwick Farm Racecourse in Sydney, Australia, on October 10, 1993. The record attendance at this one-day-only barbecue was 44,158 people! The hungry masses devoured more than 300,000 sausages, 100,000 steaks, and 50,000 chicken burgers at the **LARGEST BARBECUE**.

TRIVIA TIDBITS
The **GREATEST QUANTITY OF MEAT CONSUMED AT A BARBECUE** was 48,700 pounds of chicken, which was cooked and consumed in 8 hours at the Lancaster Sertoma Club Chicken Bar-B-Que, Lancaster, Pennsylvania, on May 18, 1996.

DID YOU KNOW?
In America, cowboys began barbecuing food in the 1880s on cattle drives in the West.

FASTEST EATER

Your nose becomes more aware of food odors when you're hungry. Imagine having terrible eyesight and living in a dark cave. How would you ever find enough food to survive? Your other senses would have to become highly developed. The star-nosed mole (*Condylura cristata*) lives under these conditions, and its amazing 22-tentacled snout always keeps its stomach full.

Dr. Kenneth Catania at Vanderbilt University, Tennessee, studied the feeding habits of the star-nosed mole using a high-speed video recorder. His published findings in February 2005 brought the nosy mammal more attention and a Guinness World Record. Its unusually shaped pink nose is the most sensitive mammal touch organ. This strange-looking snout is five times more sensitive than our fingers, and its flexible feelers aid the **FASTEST EATER** in handling small prey — such as worms, insects, and crustaceans. The star-nosed mole can identify, capture, and consume meals within 120 to 230 milliseconds!

TRIVIA TIDBITS

The star-nosed mole's teeth are perfectly formed for its fast mini-meals. It has tiny incisors, able to grasp small prey as precisely as a pair of tweezers.

Quiz Me!

Test your *Extreme!* know-how with these cool quiz questions!

Q. #75
Why is it so important to human beings that an earthworm eats its own weight in food every day?

Q. #76
How many hair cells must an insect trigger in a row before the Venus flytrap springs its "trap"?

Q. #77
True or False? Michel Lotito, also known as Monsieur Mangetout, was inspired in his metallic dietary choices by a metal-eating goat that was also recognized with a Guinness World Record.

Q. #78
True or False? Heinz® Tomato Ketchup is suitable for diets that are kosher, vegan, vegetarian, and gluten-free.

Q. #79
A hamburger is popular around the world — except among cows. How many quarter-pound hamburger patties can be made from an average-size cow?
a) 100
b) 550
c) 720
d) 1,001

Q. #80
Calculation check: If everyone ate the same amount, how much would one person have eaten at the **Largest Barbecue** attended by 44,158 people?

Q. #81
What do Eimer's organs have to do with the star-nosed mole?

EXTREME

SURVIVORS

Many extreme people in this book were either born with or chose to develop their unusual gifts for record-breaking. The survivors in this chapter, however, found themselves in extraordinary, **LIFE-THREATENING CIRCUMSTANCES** not of their own choosing. Yet their courage and refusal to give up in the face of such odds is a testament to the sheer tenacity of the human will.

HIGHEST FALL SURVIVED WITHOUT A PARACHUTE

Vesna Vulović of Yugoslavia was 23 years old and flying high, literally, in her new job as a flight attendant for Jugoslovenski Aerotransport. Although she had not been scheduled to work on January 26, 1972, fate placed her aboard Yugoslav Air Flight 364 from Copenhagen, Denmark, to Zagreb, Croatia. A terrorist bomb exploded inside the plane as it flew over Srbská, Kamenice, Czechoslovakia (now Czech Republic). Five crew members and all 22 passengers died as the DC-9 tore apart. Vesna was trapped in the plane's tail section. Sheltering its now-unconscious passenger, the tail plummeted 33,333 feet and crashed into the frozen ground below.

Rescuers combed the countryside despite little hope of finding survivors — instead, they found Vesna, alive and in a coma. Rushed to a hospital in Ceska, Karmenice, Vesna remained unconscious for 27 days while doctors reset her fractured skull, broken vertebrae, and broken legs. She awoke, temporarily paralyzed, and remained in the hospital for 16 months. Even more miraculously, this record-holder for **HIGHEST FALL SURVIVED WITHOUT A PARACHUTE** made a full recovery, able to walk and travel, with her love of flying undiminished.

TRIVIA TIDBITS

One of Vesna Vulović's rescuers was a former nurse, Bruno Henke, who spotted Vesna among the wreckage. Bruno cleared Vesna's airways and saved her life.

LONGEST TIME SPENT ADRIFT AT SEA ALONE

A shy young man named Poon Lim from China was the first at-sea survivor. The year was 1942 and World War II raged around the world. Poon wanted to make a difference. He signed up to be the second steward aboard a ship of the UK Merchant Navy. He believed it would be a great adventure and make him a more resourceful person — and it truly did. When the S.S. *Ben Lomond* was torpedoed on November 23, 1942, the crew abandoned ship. Poon jumped into a life raft . . . and suddenly realized he was completely on his own.

Days passed, yet no rescue ship arrived. His limited supplies running low, this increasingly resourceful castaway assembled fishhooks out of nails and flashlight parts. On April 5, 1943, a Brazilian fishing boat rescued him near Salinópolis, Brazil. Poon walked ashore after a perilous and life-changing journey of 133 days — the **LONGEST TIME SPENT ADRIFT AT SEA ALONE**.

TRIVIA TIDBITS
The S.S. *Ben Lomond* was torpedoed 565 miles west of St. Paul's Rocks, off the coast of Brazil.

DID YOU KNOW?
Poon Lim even caught a seabird with his bare hands during his life-raft journey.

LONGEST TIME WITH A BULLET IN HEAD

Never try to re-create this situation! In 1942, Kolyo Tanev Kolev of Bulgaria accidentally shot himself behind his right ear with a pistol. He was only 17 years old. But Kolyo survived. Decades later, he wanted to check on his injury, and the advances made in medical technology allowed him to actually "see" the bullet in his own head. On July 5, 2003, X-rays clearly showed the bullet, still lodged at the base of his skull, an amazing 61 years later. Kolyo's initially unfortunate experience and its incredible outcome is the **LONGEST TIME WITH A BULLET IN HEAD**.

HIGHEST G-FORCE ENDURED NONVOLUNTARILY

Astronauts, fighter pilots, and Formula One race car drivers are familiar with the effects and forces of velocity upon their bodies and vehicles. Remember the drivers of the Thrust SSC? Every time the jet engine powering that supersonic car was fired up, the drivers experienced a significant change in the g-force pressure. We experience 1 g-force, the pull of gravity upon our bodies, by standing in one place. When we move, the values involved become focused on acceleration and the amount of pressure needed to propel our body mass in a straight line. Turning corners or going in circles increases the amount of g-forces required in completing the maneuver.

Racing driver David Purley of the UK survived the **HIGHEST G-FORCE ENDURED NONVOLUNTARILY** on July 13, 1977. His race car crashed during prequalifying trials for the 1977 British Grand Prix at Silverstone in Northamptonshire, UK. His car, and his body, decelerated from 108 mph to 0 mph within 26 inches. This violent change in acceleration rate resulted in 179.8 g-forces crushing against his body mass. David suffered 29 fractures, 3 dislocations, and 6 heart stoppages, and lived to talk about the experience.

TRIVIA TIDBITS

The click beetle (*Athous haemorrhoidalis*) encounters 400 g-forces, the **HIGHEST G-FORCE ENDURED BY AN INSECT**, whenever "clicking" its body in a jackknife maneuver to propel itself 11.8 inches into the air.

LONGEST TIME SURVIVED WITHOUT A PULSE

Julie Mills of Surrey, UK, was in her early twenties when she began experiencing chest pains. She thought it was muscle strain and didn't realize the most important muscle in her body was in severe trouble. A few hours later, she was in an emergency room and diagnosed with a rare, life-threatening condition called viral myocarditis. Her heart muscle was inflamed, and because it was gradually failing, her other organs were shutting down.

Doctors and patient wouldn't give up the fight. Julie was transferred to the John Radcliffe Hospital in Oxford, UK. Cardiac surgeons told her of a brand-new procedure not yet performed in the UK: For one week, an artificial heart would handle her heart's regular work while the muscle rested and repaired itself. For three days, Julie was without a pulse in her vascular system, and endured the **LONGEST TIME SURVIVED WITHOUT A PULSE** starting August 14, 1998. During this time, a nonpulsatile blood pump (AB180) supported her body's functions. Her normal heart recovered, the pump was removed, and Julie reinvigorated her life by volunteering for the organization CRY (Cardiac Risk in the Young). She helps support other people who, under the age of 35, have to deal with heart problems and the possibility of surgery.

TRIVIA TIDBITS
Six months after leaving the hospital, Julie Mills flew to the Pittsburgh manufacturing plant of the artificial heart to personally thank its creators for helping save her life.

LONGEST SURVIVAL WITH HEART OUTSIDE BODY

In medical terms, *ectopia* means an internal organ develops in a wrong location. Most of these situations occur during pregnancy as a birth defect and greatly decrease the child's chance of survival. Normally, the heart grows beneath the breastbone on the inside of the body. *Ectopia cordis* refers to the displacement of the heart organ. This condition results in the heart protruding from a gap in the chest, abdominal, or neck area. This is a birth defect with tragic outcomes for the family. Most patients do not live beyond 48 hours.

Christopher Wall of Philadelphia, Pennsylvania, was born with *ectopia cordis* on August 19, 1975. However, he is still living today with his condition and is experiencing the **LONGEST SURVIVAL WITH HEART OUTSIDE BODY**.

Quiz Me!

Test your *Extreme!* know-how with these cool quiz questions!

Q. #82
True or False? Because of proper training and safety measures, skydiving fatalities are rare.

Q. #83
Poon Lim survived the **Longest Time Adrift at Sea Alone**. What recent popular novel also features a young man adrift on a raft after his ship sinks?

Q. #84
Accidentally shooting yourself in the head is a serious trauma, and Kolyo Tanev Kolev is lucky to have lived. What industrialized country currently has the highest firearms death rate due to accidental shootings?
a) The United Kingdom
b) Canada
c) The United States of America
d) Japan

Q. #85
By standing still, you are experiencing 1 g-force. If you were orbiting Earth in space, what amount of g-forces would you experience?

Q. #86
Amazingly, Julie Mills survived three days without a pulse in her vascular system. At what age do people generally have the highest pulse rate?

Q. #87
True or False? The *ectopia cordis* that Christopher Wall was born with is more common than you would think.

EXTREME

-ISTS

Every animal, plant, insect, tree, and human being is unique in its form, actions, and experiences. Record-breaking is all about going beyond the expected. Since humans walk across the ground on foot, why not walk on your hands underwater? You would be surprised at your own abilities and might invent a brand-new category. Such were the achievements of these record-holders on **EXTREME QUESTS** of personal excellence.

MOST PROLIFIC RECORD-BREAKER

If there is one person in the entire world *guaranteed* to have a record featured in the yearly edition from Guinness World Records, then it is Ashrita Furman. This is the man who knows how to set and break records — around the world, underwater, or atop his chin, multiple and simultaneous, in categories not even thought about before he made his attempt. He is the **MOST PROLIFIC RECORD-BREAKER**, with more than 100 records set or broken, and the holder of 38 current records. . . and he's still going strong!

Ashrita looks like an average 50-year-old man living in Jamaica, New York. But beneath his everyday exterior beats the heart of a strong-willed, imaginative competitor who holds the **MOST INDIVIDUAL RECORDS** and has set a different record on every continent!

Although he says he was never good at sports in school, he has managed to travel up Canada's CN Tower on a pogo stick. He began training and improving upon his body's endurance levels during meditation studies with Indian holy man Sri Chinmoy. His teacher inspired Ashrita to compete against himself in achieving his highest potential. In 2006, he hopped on one foot for 1 mile in 27 minutes 51 seconds. This most recent attempt was during a visit to Malaysia, one

TRIVIA TIDBITS
Food for thought: Ashrita Furman manages a health-food store.

of many countries Ashrita has seen on his record-setting journey. For his next attempt, Ashrita plans on re-breaking some of his own records — including an underwater juggling marathon that was interrupted by a curious shark!

DID YOU KNOW?

Ashrita Furman keeps this in mind during his record attempts: "Guinness World Records says to me you can do anything if you try."

GREATEST WEIGHT BALANCED ON THE HEAD

Many jobs in life help prepare us for future situations. Often, we discover our talents while performing a simple task, such as moving a stack of bricks from the left side to the right side of a construction site. Professional head-balancer John Evans didn't know — at age 18 and carrying those bricks — that years from then he would be touring the globe, delighting thousands of people from different cultures with his unique talents. But what he *did* know in that precise moment was if he could carry double the amount of bricks, then he would save time and earn more money. He discovered his talent for head-balancing when he placed a stack of bricks atop a special hat, called a "hod," and began walking. . . slowly and carefully, from one end of that construction site to the other. During this now-legendary moment, John stepped across the line between ordinary person and extraordinary record-breaker.

John could stack all 10 of the Guinness World Records he currently holds in 11 categories and balance them atop his head — but paper, even framed, is too lightweight for him. Instead, he balanced 62 *Guinness World Records* books in a 73-inch high column. A solidly built man at a height of 6 feet 1 inch and weight of 343 pounds, his strength resides in his 24-inch thick neck. John has kept milk crates, footballs, books, and even a car aloft, but the **GREATEST WEIGHT BALANCED ON THE HEAD** involved those old familiar building blocks! On December 24, 1997, he balanced 101 bricks totaling a weight of 416 pounds for 10 seconds. The event occurred at the BBC Television Centre in London.

People willingly climb inside boats or onto chairs to be lifted into the air by John. He managed a record load of eager fans, balancing (individually) 92 people on his head for at least 10 seconds each over the course of one hour. On July 23, 2000 at the Lowestoft Motorcycle Show in Lowestoft, UK, John set the record for **HEAVIEST COMBINED WEIGHT BALANCED ON THE HEAD IN ONE HOUR**. In the 60-minute span, a whopping total weight of 11,420 pounds moved onto and off John's sturdy skull!

HEAVIEST AIRCRAFT PULLED BY AN INDIVIDUAL

Australian David Huxley would not object to being called a "plane" kind of guy. This strongman extraordinaire taxied planes down the runway using only his body, a rope, and a towing harness strapped around his shoulders, waist, and legs. Plane-pulling since 1991, David worked his way through a fleet of aircraft. By the age of 39, he had pulled, *individually*, different models of the Boeing 747 series to the Concorde.

The **HEAVIEST AIRCRAFT PULLED BY AN INDIVIDUAL** was a Boeing 747-400. The plane weighed 187 tons. David hauled it a total distance of 298 feet 6 inches in 1 minute 27.7 seconds. This amazing feat of strength happened on October 15, 1997, in Sydney, Australia.

David's four-month fitness regime prior to a pulling event was only part of his successful formula. His self-confidence and focus helped him imagine that the vehicle was merely an extension of his body and he needed to move it!

TRIVIA TIDBITS

Today, David Huxley applies his talents to pushing and inspiring others in achieving their own goals. He founded the Australian-based Tartan Warriors, an event-management and public-relations company specializing in the promotion of strength competitions.

DID YOU KNOW?

David Huxley didn't use his teeth when tugging a ship loaded with 175 cars *plus* people for 23 feet in Rostock, Germany. The **HEAVIEST BOAT PULLED** was the *Delphin* at 2,217,847 pounds on November 19, 1998.

MOST ELASTIC MAN

Can you touch your toes without bending your knees? How about a back bend or a leg split? These acrobatic skills are used by gymnasts and circus performers. Some people are born more flexible than others, but none more so than the **MOST ELASTIC MAN**.

Pierre Beauchemin was the ultimate performer. He loved stretching his body — along with his cheering fans' imaginations. This skilled contortion artist performed under the stage name of "Mr. Gumby." His repertoire of oversplitting, front- and back-bending, and body-squeezing stunts appeared to be endless, until his death from an unrelated illness, on November 4, 2000.

Pierre's parents discovered his talent when he was only a year old. He did not have any disease or rare skin condition or birth defect. He willfully dislocated his joints, a highly unusual and painful trick. Doctors told Pierre to stop or he would be disabled by the age of 30. Pierre knew their advice was wrong, so he turned around and walked away. . . backward. In 1999, Pierre astonished the studio and viewing audience of *Guinness World Records: Primetime* by dislocating both legs before squeezing inside a box the same size as a picnic basket (29 X 15 X 15 inches).

STRETCHIEST SKIN

Ehlers-Danlos Syndrome is a rare medical condition affecting the connective tissues, elasticity of the skin, and mobility of the joints. The skin's collagen becomes defective, resulting in a loosening of the skin. Some contortion artists are afflicted with this disorder and turn it into a performance advantage. Pierre Beauchemin (see page 132) did not have this syndrome. But another two-time record-holder living with this condition relies upon his skin's enhanced elasticity to help him reach beyond previously set category limits.

On October 29, 1999, Garry Turner of Caistor, UK, proved he has the **STRETCHIEST SKIN**. The studio and viewing audiences of *Guinness World Records: Primetime* taped in Los Angeles, California, witnessed Garry stretch the skin of his stomach to an incredible length of 6.25 inches.

The temporary discomfort caused during his record attempts is not enough to deter Garry from sharing his famous record of **MOST CLOTHESPINS CLIPPED ON A FACE**. On November 27, 2004, Garry attached a total of 159 ordinary wooden clothespins to every available inch of his face skin during the Guinness World Records 2005 Roadshow at the Trafford Centre, Manchester, UK. This demonstration eclipsed his previous record of 154 clothespins!

DID YOU KNOW?

Inventor David M. Smith of Springfield, Vermont, patented the first spring clothespin in 1853. The Shakers are credited with the invention of the original wooden clothespeg during the 1800s.

TRIVIA TIDBITS

Garry Turner's favorite trick is to stretch the skin of his neck over his mouth to create the "human turtleneck." He demonstrated his skills to passersby on London's Millennium Bridge in celebration of Guinness World Records' 50th anniversary.

FULL BODY ICE CONTACT ENDURANCE

TRIVIA TIDBITS

Wim Hof wore protective eye goggles during his second ice-swimming attempt because his retinas had frozen during his first attempt. Unable to see, Wim nearly missed the hole cut into the ice for his safe exit from the dangerous waters.

DID YOU KNOW?

Skin temperature depends on air chill factors and the environment. Normal skin temperature is around 91 degrees Fahrenheit.

Wim Hof of the Netherlands has a warm personality, but operates at a colder body temperature of 95 degrees Fahrenheit — especially when he demonstrates his shiver-inducing skills. Wim holds two Guinness World Records for becoming a human ice cube — standing in an ice-filled transparent tube and swimming beneath arctic waters. He uses yoga and breathing exercises to help his body prepare for the extreme temperature changes. The dangers of frostbite are minimal in comparison with the danger of heart and organ failure. Doctors have been present at all of his attempts, yet Wim has never suffered from any of these conditions.

The record for **FULL BODY ICE CONTACT ENDURANCE** requires the participant to have direct, full-body contact with the ice. On September 11, 2004, Wim climbed into the tube, wearing only swimming trunks, and stood among the ice cubes for 1 hour 8 minutes, beating his previous record by 56 seconds. This event occurred on the set of the TV show *Guinness World Records: 50 Years, 50 Records* in London. His second record for **LONGEST SWIM UNDER ICE (BREATH HELD)** was set on March 16, 2000. He dove into a lake near Kolari, Finland, and swam 188 feet 6 inches beneath 3 feet of ice, wearing only goggles and swim trunks.

Wim believes his feats of endurance strengthen the connection between mind and body and hopes his accomplishments will help other people realize that they are capable of achieving far more than they may have thought possible.

Quiz Me!

Test your *Extreme!* know-how with these cool quiz questions!

Q. #88
Ashrita Furman climbed the CN Tower on a pogo stick. What famous Japanese mountain has he also climbed using a pogo stick?

Q. #89
True or False? In many African societies, women can carry 70 percent of their body weight on their heads.

Q. #90
True or false? David Huxley holds strongman records for pulling planes and lifting boats.

Q. #91
True or False? Double-jointed people like Pierre Beauchemin have more joints than other people.

Q. #92
Garry Turner has Ehlers-Danlos Syndrome, making his skin's collagen defective. Which of the following are also conditions that result from defective collagen?
a) Influenza
b) Acute nasopharyngitis
c) Osteogenesis imperfecta
d) None of the above

Q. #93
Wim Hof has practiced his skill long enough to never suffer from frostbite. Which of the following are warning signs of frostbite?
a) The affected area becomes numb.
b) Skin feels rock hard.
c) Skin appears waxy, white, or grayish.
d) All of the above

Quizzed Out!

At the end of each chapter was a challenge of your record-breaking smarts. Check your **ANSWERS** against the real facts listed below.

EXTREME SKILLS

Q. #1
Answer: "b," John Montagu, 4th Earl of Sandwich. In the eighteenth century, John Montagu, 4th Earl of Sandwich, wanted to continue playing cards while eating, so he asked that the meat he had been eating with his bare hands be put between two slices of bread — and from that, we have the sandwich!

Q. #2
Answer: False. The "World Toe Wrestling Organization" has tried to qualify for the Olympics, but so far, it has been unsuccessful.

Q. #3
Answer: Surfing began in Hawaii. In 1778, members of Captain Cook's third expedition to the Pacific wrote accounts of seeing islanders surfing. However, surfing is believed to have been practiced by native Hawaiians since the fifteenth century.

Q. #4
Answer: Llanwrtyd Wells is called "The Smallest Town in Britain," with a population of about 600 people.

Q. #5
Answer: Hydrobikes.

Q. #6
Answer: "d," All of the above. A "flamingo" is standing up on your seat while doing a wheelie, an "endo" is applying the front brakes while moving to bring the back tire off the ground, and a "wheelie" is using the bike's motor to bring the front tire off of the ground. Don't try these at home!

Q. #7
Answer: Yes! In 1943, Maria Dickin (the founder of People's Dispensary for Sick Animals, a United Kingdom veterinary charity) set up the "Dickin Medal" as an award for any animal displaying conspicuous gallantry and devotion to duty while serving with armed forces or civil emergency services. Between 1943 and 1949, PDSA awarded 54 Dickin Medals to 32 pigeons, 18 dogs, 3 horses, and 1 cat.

Q. #8
Answer: "d," All of the above.

Q. #9
Answer: True. The Winter X Games are currently held in Aspen, Colorado, and officially began in 1997.

EXTREME KILLERS

Q. #10
Answer: Only one. In 2003, a biologist was dragged underwater by a leopard seal while snorkeling near an Antarctic research station.

Q. #11
Answer: True.

Q. #12
Answer: No. In fact, only about 15 percent of all snake species have venom that is harmful or fatal to human beings.

Q. #13
Answer: "a," 2. The Gila lizard and the Mexican beaded lizard are the only poisonous lizards we currently know about.

Q. #14
Answer: "d," None of the above. The cassowary is actually a shy bird. It can't fly and its diet consists mainly of fruit.

Q. #15
Answer: "d," More than 10,000. Amazingly, scientists are always finding new ant species in the world.

Q. #16
Answer: True. By hitching rides on cargo ships in bunches of bananas, this spider truly does wander!

EXTREME DANGER

Q. #17
Answer: The black widow spider. The female black widow often kills and eats the male after mating (hence the spider's name). And the male brown antechini thought they had it rough!

Q. #18
Answer: Indeed. A traditional Japanese verse is: "Last night he and I ate fugu; today I help carry his coffin"!

Q. #19
Answer: No. Sometimes rattlesnakes give off a warning rattle, and sometimes they don't.

Q. #20
Answer: The International Brotherhood of Magicians, which is the world's largest organization for magicians, with nearly 15,000 members worldwide. Check it out at www.magician.org.

Q. #21
Answer: True. When carbon dioxide erupted from Lake Nyos on August 21, 1986, the denser gas spilled into the surrounding valley and suffocated thousands of animals and people.

Q. #22
Answer: "d," 0. Thankfully, at this time, there have been no outbreaks of the Ebola virus in the US.

EXTREME SPEED

Q. #23
Answer: True. Grass is the largest irrigated crop in the US, beating out corn by three times. Good thing those lawn mowers can move so fast!

Q. #24
Answer: "b," the Murphy Bed. The Murphy Bed is a bed that folds down from a wall. William L. Murphy applied for a patent for this idea April 1, 1916, and it's been going up and down ever since.

Q. #25
Answer: So far, not a one.

Q. #26
Answer: "d," All of the above.

Q. #27
Answer: "d," All of the above.

EXTREME ON THE MOVE

Q. #28
Answer: While a sonic boom

causes a loud noise that sounds like a clap of thunder, it cannot hurt you.

Q. #29
Answer: The Channel Tunnel, or Chunnel, is a 31-mile-long rail tunnel beneath the English Channel that connects France and the UK. A hugely expensive project that saw several false starts, it was finally completed in 1994 and is the second-longest rail tunnel in the world. Of course, you look much cooler crossing the Channel with a water-skier behind you!

Q. #30
Answer: "b," 98 percent. Because of the *Shinkai 6500*'s maximum depth limitation of 6,500 meters, most of the world's ocean floor is open to its exploration.

Q. #31
Answer: Water strider insects easily walk on water. Scientists have found that the strider's legs are covered with fine, water-resistant hairs that keep them afloat.

Q. #32
Answer: Adho Mukha Vrksasana is just the name for a handstand in yoga. Adho Mukha Vrksasana literally means Downward Facing Tree Pose. The next time your gym teacher asks if you can do a handstand, you can tell them you prefer doing the Adho Mukha Vrksasana!

Q. #33
Answer: Since their first use in 1967, the transporters have racked up 2,526 miles. About the same distance as a round-trip car ride from the Kennedy Space Center (in Florida) to New York City!

Q. #34
Answer: True! Skateboarding started in the 1950s, when some surfers got the idea of trying to "surf the streets" — and the skateboard was born.

EXTREME SOUNDS
Q. #35
Answer: False. A "black hole" is not a hole in the standard sense of the word, but only a region of outer space.

Q. #36
Answer: True. In China, burping after a meal is often seen as a sign that you've enjoyed your food.

Q. #37
Answer: "d," All of the above. You might know somnambulism better as sleepwalking, narcolepsy is falling asleep involuntarily, and bruxism is grinding your teeth when you sleep.

Q. #38
Answer: "Little Elephant Saddle," "Floating down the Pin River," "Pin Pia," "Bamboolin," "Dancing with Prathida," and "Kaw-Liga" are just 6 of the 24 tracks (songs) available on their second album, *Elephonic Rhapsodies*.

Q. #39
Answer: VJ. In the early 1980s, music videos became popular and the term "VJ," or "video jockey," was born.

Q. #40
Answer: Yodeling started in the Swiss Alps. It is believed to have been developed as a form of communication between the high mountain peaks there.

EXTREME SMELLS
Q. #41
Answer: Yes! But don't worry, there has only been one recorded instance of a polar bear killing a human in the US (Alaska). Even so, if you see a polar bear, keep your distance.

Q. #42
Answer: Pheromones are biochemicals secreted from the body that are important in communication between animals of the same species. Scientists have shown that animals use pheromones to communicate alarm, find food, mate, etc.

Q. #43
Answer: Your sense of smell is called "olfaction."

Q. #44
Answer: True! "Corpse flowers" reaching heights of more than 9 feet have been found.

Q. #45
Answer: So long ago, no one's really sure! Garlic is mentioned in the Bible, ancient Egyptians ate it while building the pyramids, and it shows up in ancient Greek literature.

EXTREME EXTENSIONS
Q. #46
Answer: Some famous polydactyls include: Anne Boleyn, the second wife of Henry VIII, who is said to have had 11 fingers; Liam Gallagher, the lead singer of Oasis, who has 6 toes on each foot; and Antonio Alfonseca, pitcher for the Florida Marlins, who has 6 fingers on each hand and 6 toes on each foot (earning him the nickname "El Pulpo," the octopus).

Q. #47
Answer: Yes. Cyrano de Bergerac has been the subject of several films, including a 1950 film starring José Ferrer, a 1990 French-language version starring Gérard Depardieu, and a comedic Hollywood version, *Roxanne*, starring Steve Martin.

Q. #48
Answer: Yes. Your inner ear contains about 30,000 or so tiny hair cells. These hair cells are extremely important because each time there is a vibration of sound, the hair cells move, and, when the hair cells move, they send a signal to your brain telling it that a sound has occurred. These little cells are vital for your hearing.

Q. #49
Answer: "d," All of the above. Gandalf, Papa Smurf, and Dumbledore may not have much in common, but they all have beards!

Q. #50
Answer: "c," A "mustachio" is a term for a large mustache.

Q. #51
Answer: Punctate leukonychia (a medical term for "white spots"). Don't worry, it may sound scary, but *punctate leukonychia* is quite common and usually harmless.

Q. #52
Answer: 136 painted their

toenails. In fact, depictions of pedi-cure-like services have been found in ancient Egyptian tombs.

Q. #53
Answer: Yes. One such culture is the Masai, a tribe in Eastern Africa. Among both Masai men and women, stretched earlobes are considered a sign of beauty.

EXTREME TEETH
Q. #54
Answer: True. If you define muscu-lar strength as the ability to exert force on an external object, the masseter is the strongest muscle. However, people sometimes claim the heart is strongest because it does more work over one's lifetime than any other muscle and is almost impossible to fatigue.

Q. #55
Answer: "d," All of the above. Halitosis is bad breath, gingivitis is inflammation of the gums, and periodontitis is bacterial infection of the gums. Brush your teeth!

Q. #56
Answer: True. Historically, dental extractions were used to treat a va-riety of illnesses. During the Middle Ages and through the nineteenth century, "barbers" would extract teeth with instruments like the "dental pelican" (which resembled a pelican's beak) or the "dental key" (which looked like a door key). Ouch!

Q. #57
Answer: Yes! Sperm whales typi-cally have a life span of 50 to 80 years — quite a long life span

considering the average American human can expect to live approxi-mately 77 years.

Q. #58
Answer: Not really. Because the gi-ant armadillo eats mainly termites and ants, its teeth are peglike; in fact, the giant armadillo completely lacks incisor or canine teeth.

Q. #59
Answer: Yes. In fact, coconut-har-vesting training schools exist for monkeys in southern Thailand. Monkeys are often considered a cost-efficient way of harvesting coconuts.

EXTREME FOOD
Q. #60
Answer: "a," Dodger Stadium. In 2005, the Los Angeles-based baseball stadium sold 1,674,400 hot dogs!

Q. #61
Answer: Two Rivers, Wisconsin, calls itself "Home of the Ice Cream Sundae." Reportedly, in 1881, a tourist visited a local soda fountain and asked for chocolate sauce to be poured over a dish of ice cream. At the time, this was considered a little bizarre. However, this "invention" soon caught on and became a huge success. But, just so you know, Evanston, Illinois, and Ithaca, New York, are among the other American cities that claim the ice cream sundae started in their town.

Q. #62
Answer: Idaho. The state pro-duces about a third of the USA's potatoes. Guess what the state

vegetable is? That's right: the potato!

Q. #63
Answer: True. Ginger can serve as a digestive aid for mild stomach upset and is commonly recom-mended by professional herbalists to help prevent or treat nausea and vomiting. (Just don't eat a whole gingerbread house.)

Q. #64
Answer: Yes. The 1962 Japanese film *King Kong vs. Godzilla* shows the two legendary screen monsters fighting each other.

Q. #65
Answer: "c," Taiwan. In 2004, one lawmaker threw her lunch box across the room at another legislator dur-ing a disagreement. That legislator retaliated, and soon the room of lawmakers began a full-scale food fight that left tabletops, chairs, and the floor littered with rice and chunks of hard-boiled eggs!

EXTREME LUXURIES
Q. #66
Answer: Besides being the **Highest Point in the World** at 29,028 feet 9 inches, Mount Everest is also dangerous to climb. More than 1,300 people have climbed Everest, but 179 people have died while at-tempting to reach its summit!

Q. #67
Answer: Yes. Having a fear of the number 13 is called triskaideka-phobia. (Even the term sounds scary!)

Q. #68
Answer: While there's no fixed rule,

longer, more complex comic books are often called graphic novels.

Q. #69
Answer: Currently, either Topps or Upper Deck produces all major league baseball cards.

Q. #70
Answer: "b," King Tyrant Lizard. Let's break down the word roots of Tyran-nosauraus Rex: *Tyrannos* is Greek for "tyrant;" the word *sauros* means "lizard," and *rex* is Latin for "king."

Q. #71
Answer: "a," Switzerland. At more than 22 pounds per year, the Swiss consume more chocolate per capita than any other nation. Compare that figure to the 11 pounds of chocolate consumed per American!

Q. #72
Answer: Check out this Web site: www.elephantart.com. This is the Internet home of the "Asian Elephant Art & Conservation Proj-ect." Here you can see a selection of art created by elephants from around the world, including the Thai Elephant Conservation Center.

Q. #73
Answer: "d," Both "a" and "b." The AIBO® comes close to a real dog — but isn't the real thing!

Q. #74
Answer: False. There are more open seats available to those who can pay the steep 20 million-dollar price tag. Save up!

EXTREME APPETITES
Q. #75
Answer: The earthworm actually

eats its way through the soil. The ingested soil is ground up and digested, and the waste deposited behind the worm. This process aerates and mixes the soil, and is considered helpful by gardeners and farmers. Research shows that in 100 square feet of garden soil, earthworms may bring from 4 to 8 pounds of dirt to the soil surface each year.

Q. #76
Answer: The trigger hairs of a Venus flytrap must be touched twice in quick succession so that non-prey stimuli, such as rain, don't falsely trigger the trap.

Q. #77
Answer: False. Goats eating metal is a myth. In fact, goats are actually quite picky eaters.

Q. #78
Answer: True!

Q. #79
Answer: "c," 720. A single cow, on average, yields enough hamburger meat to make about 720 quarter-pound hamburger patties!

Q. #80
Answer: On average, one person would have eaten: 6.8 sausages, 2.26 steaks, and 1.13 chicken burgers!

Q. #81
Answer: The star-nosed mole can eat because of the circle of 22 fleshy tentacles at the end of its snout, which are used to identify food by touch. The incredibly sensitive nasal tentacles are covered with thousands of minute touch receptors known as Eimer's organs,

first described by German zoologist Theodor Eimer.

EXTREME SURVIVORS
Q. #82
Answer: True. Despite the seeming danger of leaping out of a plane, fatalities are rare. About 30 skydivers are killed each year in the US, which works out to approximately one death out of every 100,000 jumps.

Q. #83
Answer: In Yann Martel's *Life of Pi*, an unusual young man, Pi Patel, survives on a raft with a Bengal tiger for 227 days.

Q. #84
Answer: "c," The United States of America.

Q. #85
Answer: 0 g-force. There's no gravity in space.

Q. #86
Answer: Generally, pulse rates are higher in younger people. For example, a resting heart rate for an infant is as high as, or higher, than an adult's pulse rate while doing strenuous exercise.

Q. #87
Answer: False. *Ectopia cordis* is quite rare, occurring from 5.5 to 7.9 times per 1,000,000 live births.

EXTREME-ISTS
Q. #88
Answer: Mt. Fuji, Japan's highest mountain.

Q. #89
Answer: True. In many African societies, particularly where there is no running water, women must carry buckets of water on their heads for their family's cooking, washing, and drinking. Scientists are currently studying why these women are able to carry so much with little to no additional expense of energy.

Q. #90
Answer: False. David Huxley holds two records in the vehicle-pulling (not lifting!) category.

Q. #91
Answer: False. Every fully formed person has exactly the same number of joints. "Double-jointed" people can just bend much farther than one might think a joint would allow a limb to bend.

Q. #92
Answer: "c," Osteogenesis imperfecta. You may know influenza better as the flu, and acute nasopharyngitis is just another name for the common cold. However, osteogenesis imperfecta is brittle bone disease and results from having less collagen than is normal. With brittle bone disease, people suffer from weak, fragile bones.

Q. #93
Answer: "d," All of the above. If you've been playing outside in the cold and you start feeling this way, it may be the first stage of frostbite, called "frostnip," so get inside!

Our trip together through the archives of GUINNESS WORLD RECORDS is at an end for this collection of extreme stories and statistics. Except your journey doesn't have to stop here! You can read about the experiences and see eye-popping photos of record-breakers in even more outrageous, phenomenal, and extraordinary categories in the annual edition of *Guinness World Records* or at the official online archives (www.guinnessworld records.com).

This book and its exceptional people may have inspired you to become a record-holder. Check out the official rules for making a record attempt listed in the back of the book.

We wish you good luck and always remember — every day gives you a new opportunity to do something out of the ordinary and become a record-breaker in your wonderfully unique style!

BE A RECORD-BREAKER!

MESSAGE FROM THE OFFICIAL KEEPER OF THE RECORDS:

Record-breakers are the ultimate in one way or another – the youngest, the oldest, the tallest, the smallest. So how do you get to be a record-breaker?

FOLLOW THESE IMPORTANT STEPS:

1. Before you attempt your record, check with us to make sure your record is suitable and safe. Get your parents' permission. Next, contact one of our officials by using the record application form at **www.guinnessworldrecords.com**.

2. Tell us about your idea. Give us as much information as you can, including what the record is, when you want to attempt it, where you'll be doing it, and so on.

a) We will tell you if a record already exists, what safety guidelines you must follow during your attempt to break that record, and what evidence we need as proof that you completed your attempt.

b) If your idea is a brand-new record nobody has set yet, we need to make sure it meets our requirements. If it does, then we'll write official rules specific to that record idea and make sure all attempts are made in the same way.

3. Whether it is a new or existing record, we will send you the guidelines for your selected record. Once you receive these, you can make your attempt at any time. You do not need a Guinness World Record official at your attempt. But you do need to gather evidence. Find out more about the kind of evidence we need to see by visiting our Web site.

4. Think you've already set or broken a record? Put all of your evidence as specified by the guidelines in an envelope and mail it to us at Guinness World Records.

5. Our officials will investigate your claim fully – a process that can take up to 10 weeks, depending on the number of claims we've received, and how complex your record is.

6. If you're successful, you will receive an official certificate that says you are now a Guinness World Record-holder!

Need more info? Check out the Kids' Zone on **www.guinnessworldrecords.com** for lots more hints and tips and some top record ideas that you can try at home or at school. Good luck!

Photos

The publisher would like to thank the following for their kind permission to use their photographs in this book:

6 Motorcycle Burnout © Mike Cooper/Allsport/Getty Images; 7 (top) Dave Mirra © Paul Sakuma/AP Wide World Photos; 7 (bottom), 8 Rob Williams © Brenda Ladd Photography/www.brendaladdphoto.com; 9 Toe Wrestling Championship © Neale Haynes/REX USA; 10 Dale Webster © Christopher Chung/Santa Rosa Press Democrat; 11 Bog Snorkeling © David Jones/AP Wide World Photos; 12 Vittorio Innocente Courtesy of Guinness World Records; 13 Dave Mirra © Mark J. Terrill/AP Wide World Photos; 14 Ron and Brutus © Tom Sanders/Aerial Focus; 15 Augie © 2005 Drew Gardner/Guinness World Records; 16 Motorcycle Burnout © Miguel Riopa/AFP/Getty Images; 18 (left) Huntsman Spider © Gerry Ellis/Minden Pictures; 18 (right), 24 Gila Monster © Tim Flach/Stone/Getty Images; 19 Leopard Seal © Kevin Schafer/CORBIS; 20 Adelie Penguin on Leopard Seal © Tim Davis/CORBIS; 21 Sea Wasp © Gary Bell/ Taxi/Getty Images; 23 Small-Scaled Snake © Cliff Frith/Bruce Coleman USA; 25 Cassowary Bird © Peter Arnold, Inc.; 26 (top) Bulldog Ant © Christoph Hellhake/Stone/Getty Images, (bottom) Wandering Spider © Ken Preston-Mafham/Animals Animals - Earth Scenes; 28 Jackie Bibby © Ellis Neel/Alamogordo Daily News/AP Wide World Photos; 29 (left), 31 Puffer Fish © Jeffrey L. Rotman/CORBIS; 29 (right) Brown Antechinus © Ralph & Daphne Keller/Natural History Photo Archive; 30 Brown Antechinus © Prenzel Photo/Animals Animals - Earth Scenes; 32 Jackie Bibby © 2005 Drew Gardner/Guinness World Records; 33 MTK Courtesy of Matthew Cassiere/www.MattTheKnife.com; 34 (left) Ebola Virus SEM Image © Scott Camazine/Alamy, (right) Lake Nyos © Peter Turnley/CORBIS; 36 Florence Griffith Joyner © Susan Sterner/AP Wide World Photos; 37 (top) Cockroach Racing © Daniel Hulshizer/AP Wide World Photos; 37 (bottom), 38 Lawn Mower Racer © Benjamin Porter; 39 Casual Lofa © David Davenport 1999/cummfybanana.co.uk; 41 (left) Florence Griffith Joyner © AP Wide World Photos, (right) Asafa Powell © Thanassis Stavrakis/AP Wide World Photos; 42 (top) Midge On Water © Elisabeth Sauer/zefa/CORBIS, (bottom) Cockroach Pulling Toy Tractor Courtesy of Purdue University; 44 (left) Aquada Car © Ben Stansall/REX USA; 44 (right), 50 Biggest Skateboard Courtesy of Foundation Skateboards; 45 Thrust SSC © Yousef Allan/AP Wide World Photos; 46 Thrust SSC at Black Rock Desert © Reuters; 47 Sealegs Vehicle Courtesy of Sealegs International Ltd.; 48 (top) Remy Bricka © Vince Bucci/AFP/Getty Images, (bottom) Boy Handstands © Jeffrey L. Rotman/CORBIS; 49 *Discovery* Shuttle on Launch Pad © NASA; 52 (top) Yodeling Festival © Reuters/Newscom, (bottom) Disc Jockey Mixing © Daly & Newton /Stone/Getty Images; 54 Perseus Cluster © NASA; 55 Paul Hunn © Ray Tang/REX USA; 56 Bullhorn © Matt Knannlein/iStockphoto; 57 Elephant Orchestra © Jason Reed/Reuters/Landov; 58 (top) Yahoo Yodelers Courtesy of Guinness World Records, (bottom) Disc jockey Overhead View © Antonio Luiz Hamdan /Photographer's Choice/Getty Images; 60 *Amorphophallus Titanium* © Tony Larkin/REX USA; 61 (left) Polar Bear Standing © Steven Kazlowski/Peter Arnold, Inc.; 61 (right), 66 (bottom) Gilroy Garlic Festival © Marcio Jose Sanchez/AP Wide World Photos; 62 Polar Bear Walking © Agliolo/Yarnell/Index Stock Imagery/Jupiter Images; 63 Polyphemus Moth © Jeff Lepore/Photo Researchers, Inc.; 64 Hill Top Research Labs © AP/Wide World Photos; 65 *Amorphophallus Titanium* © Dan Chung/Reuters/CORBIS; 66 (top) Gilroy Garlic Ice Cream Stand © Robert Holmes/CORBIS; 68 (left) Tribhuwan Yadav Courtesy of Guinness World Records, (right) Mehmet Ozyurek © Agence France Presse/Newscom; 69 Long-Haired Man © Thanh Nien/AP Wide World Photos; 70 Polydactylism © Dr. M.A. Ansary/Photo Researchers, Inc.; 71 Mehmet Ozyurek © ZUMA Press/Newscom; 73 Radhakant Bajpai Courtesy of Guinness World Records; 74 Antanas Kontrimas Courtesy of Guinness World Records; 75 Ram Singh Chauhan © Sherwin Crasto/AP Wide World Photos; 76 Lee Redmond © 2004 Drew Gardner/Guinness World Records; 77 Louise Hollis Courtesy of Guinness World Records; 78 Monte Pierce Courtesy of Guinness World Records; 80 Giant Armadillo © Paul Crum/Photo Researchers, Inc.; 81 (left), 86 (right) Sidaraju S. Raju Courtesy of Guinness World Records; 81 (right), 129 (inset) Great White Shark © Mike Parry/Minden Pictures; 82 Dusky Shark © Ron & Valerie Taylor/SeaPics.com; 84 Omar Hanapiev Courtesy of Guinness World Records; 85 Sperm Whale © Francois Gohier/Photo Researchers, Inc.; 86 (left) Giant Armadillo © Gabriel Rojo/Nature Picture Library; 88 (right) Hotdog © Vienna Beef Via Getty Images; 90 Longest Hotdog Courtesy of Conshohocken Italian Bakery; 88 (left), 92 Gingerbread Giant Courtesy of Hyatt Regency Hotel Vancouver/Guinness World Records; 89, 93 Popcorn Kong © Tony Kyriacou/REX USA; 91 Bernd Sikora Courtesy of Guinness World Records; 94 Tomatina © Heino Kalis/Reuters; 96 (top), 104 Elephant Painters Courtesy of Guinness World Records; 96 (bottom) Diamond © Matthias Kulka/CORBIS; 97 Money © JLP/Deimos/zefa/CORBIS; 98 Henry Shelford Courtesy of Guinness World Records; 99 Lamborghini © Daniel Boschung/zefa/CORBIS; 100 Pay Copy *Marvel Comics No. 1* © Marvel Entertainment, Inc.; 101 T206 Honus Wagner © Kathy Willens/AP Wide World Photos; 102 Sue the T-Rex © Mike Derer/AP Wide World Photos; 103 Scott Expedition Chocolate © Max Nash/AP Wide World Photos; 105 TMSUK-4 © Toshifumi Kitamura/AP Wide World Photos; 106 Dennis Tito © Russian Space Agency/AP Wide World Photos; 108 (left) C. Manoharan Snake Flossing © JAY/EPA/Landov, (right) Carnivorous Plant © Michel Viard/Peter Arnold, Inc.; 109 Star-Nosed Mole © Rod Planck/Photo Researchers, Inc.; 110 C. Manoharan © Ananthakrishnan AH/TW/Reuters; 111 Venus Flytrap © M. & C. Photography/Peter Arnold, Inc.; 113 Monsieur Mangetout © LVS/REX USA; 114 (left) Johnny Reitz, (right) Dustin Phillips Courtesy of Guinness World Records; 115 BBQ Meat © iStockphoto; 116 Star-Nosed Mole © Gary Meszaros/Photo Researchers, Inc.; 118 (left) Poon Lim Courtesy of Poon Lim/from *Sole Survivor* by Ruthanne Lum McCunn; 118 (right) Human Heart © Don Farrall/Photodisc/Getty Images; 119, 122 X-Rays from Kolyo Tanev Kolev Courtesy of Guinness World Records; 120 Vesna Vulovic © Libor Zavoral/AFP/Newscom; 121 Poon Lim Aboard Raft © SF Stanley/US NAVY, courtesy of Ruthanne Lum McCunn; 123 David Purley © Paul Brooks/REX USA; 124 (top) Julie Mills Courtesy of Cardiac Risk in the Young: C-R-Y.org.uk, (bottom) Human Heart Clip Art; 126 (left), 128, 129 Ashrita Furman © 2004 Drew Gardner/Guinness World Records; 126 (right), 130 John Evans © 2001 Drew Gardner/Guinness World Records; 127 David Huxley Courtesy of Guinness World Records; 131 David Huxley © 2006 David Anderson/Guinness World Records; 132 Pierre Beauchemin © Michel Bontemp/PONOPRESSE; 133 Garry Turner © 2001 Drew Gardner/Guinness World Records; 134 Wim Hof © TF1/SIPA Press.

Index

143